Samuel Bowles

Golden gleams from the heavenly light

Samuel Bowles

Golden gleams from the heavenly light

ISBN/EAN: 9783337270209

Printed in Europe, USA, Canada, Australia, Japan

Cover: Foto ©Andreas Hilbeck / pixelio.de

More available books at **www.hansebooks.com**

GOLDEN GLEAMS

FROM

THE HEAVENLY LIGHT.

BY

SPIRIT SAMUEL BOWLES.

[Late Editor Springfield (Mass) Republican.]

Mrs. Carolinu E. S. Twing, Medium.

ISSUED BY

THE STAR PUBLISHING COMPANY,

91 Sherman St.,

SPRINGFIELD, MASS.

Price 30 Cents, Postage, Free.

DEDICATION.

To the rank and file of humanity, seeking for a glimpse of the kingdom of Truth, I dedicate this book.

SAMUEL BOWLES.

INTRODUCTION.

In all the efforts I have made for the enlightenment of the people of earth on spiritual lines of thought, I have never sent out a book which carried with it a stronger prayer for investigation than this.

I know it will meet opposition and ridicule from a public, waiting to criticise and laugh down all efforts of those called dead, to reach it.

I know religious bigots will frown it down and label it dangerous.

I know the lady, whose hand I used, will by some, be held responsible, when even many of the sentiments expressed, are not at all in line with her way of thinking

I know a conspiracy of silence regarding it will as formerly, be maintained in one direction.

I know it will be declared unlike my former style—less graphic, and lacking in many of the attributes which the world is now pleased to say I once possessed.

These opinions may in some measure, be true; but I would like to have this test applied: read to some competent person, an extract from my best earthly writing, either editorial or descriptive, and then one of the best extracts from this book, and see if an unprejudiced mind will not perceive a similarity in the two—the first written when I used my own hand—this book, written, often under great difficulty, when I used the hand of another.

I send this little book out on a mission. The others have produced results far beyond my hopes and expectations. I send this out as a protest against the unbelief which will not recognize in the Infinite, a controlling power, which can always keep the spiritual world watching and guarding the material world.

SAMUEL BOWLES.

PAPER I.

A Visit to an Art Gallery in Heaven.

Mary said to me one morning, "Samuel, let us do something human, let us visit the art gallery you were invited to visit sometime ago, and learn to love the heavenly pictures as we loved the earthly ones, crude though they would seem to us now."

So we started out from our happy home, leaving the doors wide open—no fear of thieves here. We passed by homes where the voices of children were heard in song—we passed by gatherings where abstruse questions were being discussed—we saw bands of anxious-looking spirits, speeding away to be in time at some death-bed scene in earth life. But there was no crowding; no one was seeking a bargain counter; no one wanted an electric car; no one was in a rush for a train; but every one was eager that the hours should bring something to their soul-life.

"Do you want to go with me?" asked Mary; "now I think of it, I remember you were not very much impressed by pictures in the old life."

"Yes, I want to go. I loved beauty and art, but I was obliged to subordinate them to the practical utilities of life. I had but little time for esthetic musings. I lived among disenchanting, common place realities; and you see the effect of it now. I can report a meeting of any kind, but I cannot describe this heavenly scenery, or half do justice to one leaf or flower."

"I think you do very nicely," said my comforter.

We had now come to the gallery—an immense structure of what seemed to be white cut glass which alternated with blocks of murky whiteness. The effect was very beautiful; but the roof was the culmination of architecture, and although of the same material, it was gathered together like a cloth drapery around a common center and culminated in the immense tower from which waves of light of changing hue, illuminated the interior. This vast structure was divided by great archways, making different apartments for the different classes of pictures.

The pictures in the first department were painted by those who had in earth life so longed to copy nature, but whose hands were tied; those whose days were filled with hard labor and whose nights gave but little rest, and with sad longings for days that would never come in earth life. There were hundreds of pictures which looked more like living scenes in nature than like pictures.

One that particularly enchained our attention was a flower scene, where different kinds of flowers were grouped without the least inharmony in coloring—no color challenged another color to hide from a superior beauty. All was perfect harmony.

I noticed my wife, edging up to the picture and looking around to see if any one objected, she put her white hand upon a rose bud. "Oh! It is on a flat surface after all," said she; "I was sure it was raised; I thought I could pick that bud."

There were pictures of homes where all was

happiness—of laughing children and of happy parents—pictures of landscapes that made one almost smell the new-mown hay, or hear the tinkle of the cow bell in the adjoining pasture—pictures of dashing waves against rock-bound coasts—of mountains, towering in the distance—of sheep, grazing on the plain—of the thatched roof of some home, well loved by earthly association—pictures of wonderful chasms, the result of the convulsions of nature—pictures of happy boyhood, with clothes torn and with bare feet, out in the rain, trying to catch some ducks to bring them in out of the wet—pictures that told of hope long deferred and trust that would not be dismayed—of death there and life here.

I speak in the plural, because every picture had a companion piece of the same character, painted by different artists to show the status of power possessed by the artists.

"These pictures are only the early efforts of these artists," said a gentleman standing by. "They have done very creditable work since."

"Creditable work!" said my wife, her eyes wide open in wonder. "What do you call these, when I reach out to pick a rosebud, and bend my head to hear the murmur of a stream? See the limbs of those trees, swaying in the breeze. I think I hear the noise and they seem to move."

"It is an illusion, caused by the light thrown upon them from the main tower," replied he; and the sound, madam, I think that must have been an illusion."

"No, it is not," she stoutly maintained.

"Come a little farther beyond this archway,"

said our friend. As we reached the place, we were in the midst of those pictures which have been symbols of the world's slavery for centuries—the Nazarine and his life work. There were the wise men kneeling on the sand in the desert, watching for the star—the Egyptian, the Hindu and the Greek. In the dim distance, a faint outline of their waiting camels could be seen. Their faces are lighted by the radience of the new star which should lead them on.

Then the manger and child; a little way from Joseph and Mary, under the same covering are cattle, peacefully standing, not knowing they had shared their covering with one destined to be a Teacher of the world. Then comes the scene in the Temple when the boy of twelve years confounded all his questioners. The artist had put such an intense expression into his face and such a look of astonishment into the faces of those who questioned, that they seemed to be living, breathing people of that age.

Then came the multitude on the mountain side—the baptism by John and the dove descending—the wedding feast—the conversation at the well with the woman of Samaria—the healing touch—the pool of Bethesda—his arraignment before Pilot—the last supper—up Calvary's heights—on the cross—angels at the tomb—the stone rolled away—his appearance after the crucifixion.

In every picture, the face of the Nazarine was a speaking face: the faces of his enemies were black with hate, and the pitying ones who followed even to the cross, had tears on their cheeks which seemed about to drop.

My wife stood there with eyes bedimmed in tears. "Mary," said I, "This man who suffered, helped us all by his example of patience; but so has every good man and good woman who has worked for a cause that meant redemption from any sin that binds us."

"But his life was so unlike all other lives," said she. I did not argue the question with her. I had noticed that on one side a drapery covered a picture and had not thought best to raise it, but the friend who had still lingered near, came forward and raising it, showed the most beautiful conception yet of "the man of sorrow."

Hard headed as I am, I felt like bowing at the shrine of that art which could put so much expression into one face; so much of strength and so much of living love. The clear eyes seemed to read us through and through. I could sympathise with Mary when she said, "I am the way, the truth and the life."

"You have not all the thought of the artist yet," said the guide;" and he slipped aside a little pannel and we beheld in illuminated letters—"The Redeemer of the world is not Egyptian, Hindu, Greek or Hebrew; but is with the human, the building up of character from lessons of both ancient teachers and present helpers to that degree of excellence which is saving in itself."

Mary turned away with a disappointed look, and said, "Oh! who could spoil that wondrous picture by such heresy? He died to redeem the world."

I did not argue with her; but we passed along to the work of the old masters—wonderful in execution, remarkable in coloring, with no coarseness of texture visible on near approach, but still they did not chain my wife's attention like those just seen.

The apartments of Buddha and Mohammend had also their pictures—wonderful in design; telling the history of the bondage of millions of people. But their superstitions seemed so strange to Mary and I, while ours was so near to our lives.

"Why are such ideas kept up?" I asked. "They only end in bitter disappointment."

The guide replied, "They are yet necessary as an education to those who have lived in that realm. If these devotional spirits had not had the chance to bring out their ideas of Jesus, they would never have touched their brushes to canvas. Souls must find expression there or here. The pent-up lives of those who are reverent, talented and children of genius, must find expression. It would be like leaving something out of their lives, when they have lived in the love of an ideal, to forbid such expression. We daily see here what working out one's salvation means. It is uphill work. Nature's students are happiest: they hear whispers from the lips of the granite rocks they are painting. They find flowers, the chalices of divine workmanship. They revel in the pleasure of painting Alpine glaciers with fragile flowers shuddering upon the verge of eternal snow. They make the willow touch the stream and then smile at the study they have in the limped water. They chain the animals to them by links of love and then glory in the light which shines from their velvet eyes."

"But does it pay," I asked him, "when so many

stern duties are pressing upon us, to give so much time to art?"

"Think back," he said, "that is an expression of earth: you are in eternity now, and it is all yours. Let the dreamer dream; the student pursue his studies: the reformer work out the grand possibilities of his life: the singer waken the echoes of heaven: nothing can be wasted. All these experiences have their bearing upon the life of the individual, and we are in a land of individual rights."

We went home, and Mary went at once to her room. I did not follow her; I knew that which was fighting for the ascendency in her mind, and I knew she would make a wise choice between reason and superstition.

S. BOWLES.

PAPER II.

UNION MEETING OF THE CLERGY.

"Well, I would not miss attending this convention on any account," said I to my wife, as we were conversing upon other subjects, and was interrupted by the clear voice of a child, saying, "Union meeting of the clergy at the Great Temple; all invited."

We had no great preparations to make." Mary did not need a maid, nor I a man to assist in getting ready. While going there, Mary said, "It is so nice to have the clergy meet together in harmony. How different from the old life it will be!"

But I said, "Wait and see."

When we entered the Temple, we were greeted by such music as made us both pause and bow our heads. If it was an organ which produced those sounds of harmony, it had but little resemblance to the organs of the old life, and the organist must have had large experience in both sides of life, beside having a gift from high heaven. The sounds rose up as if in praise and adoration, clear and sweet as the voice of happy childhood, then sank into minor notes that told of triumph through suffering, then were heard the deep tones of strength, followed by those of victory!

I never shall know the name of the music rendered that day, for when I asked, the answer was, "It is the story of a life, told in music, and the musician was not known in earth life, only as an amateur performer."

When we at last obtained a seat in the crowded Temple, I looked around in wonder, and said to Mary, "See the interest manifested in this work." The great platform was full of men, and women too; even the galleries were packed with fair women, mostly dressed in white, and strong-looking men, dressed in the simple garb of this realm.

Henry Ward Beecher was chairman of the meeting. He arose and asked all to join in singing a hymn, beginning with

"Rejoice, rejoice, the victory will be won."

They all seemed to know the words except my wife and I and all could sing too—an attribute of this life is singing with the voice as well as a song in the soul.

As they did not open with prayer, and went at once about their business, Mary said, "They have forgotten to pray."

"I presume it is not forgotten, dear, "said I, "perhaps they are going to work out their prayers."

Mr. Beecher said, "The object of this meeting is to produce a union "of thought about essentials, by which we may better give impressions to the people of earth and not transmit so many varying ideas as are now being given; also the dropping of old credal systems, which mean bondage. We have present, I believe, people of all shades of thought, who are in earnest in their desires to teach our earth friends how to eliminate from their present creeds those dogmas that are heavy weights to them if they desire freedom. I will not say much more now. For years I have been manipulating the brain of Lyman Abbott, and now I know that I have succeeded, for from my old pulpit he is preaching words of deliverance. No more is the bloody history of a bloody and licentious age, put before the people as the work or inspiration of the Divine Being. No more are they taught to accept anything without adequate reason.

I want to ask you, my brethren, what are you doing for the emancipation of your different churches? I will first call upon Father Ryan, who is still remembered on earth, more for the truths he taught in glorious song, written in such varied ways, and under such varied circumstances that it touched hearts more than all his church work ever did.

What are you striving to eliminate from your old Catholic views to help the world?"

FATHER RYAN, THE POET PRIEST.

A strange smile passed over his dreamy face. "I almost think I am anxious to eliminate the whole church," replied he and then he added, "How terrible, oh! how terrible the whole plan, based on an unnatural birth—making the mother an unwedded woman—making the father one who did not care for virtue—making the mother more of a God than the son, and placing before the ignorant, a scapegoat for all bad actions.

The church! what would I not do for it? I would banish confession, extirminate the thought of prayers being paid for, to help friends through purgatory, throw open the doors of every convent and let the world know what dens of wickedness they are: I would hurl from the pulpit, the coarse, drinking men who minister to the people, and put them with pick and shovel, in the ditch where they belong; I would educate the people of my old church, aye, educate them so they would no more be subject to their present thralldom. I would sing songs of freedom and give to the world the rosary of years, passed under heaven's blest dome—years, in which the individual is responsible, and not the church.

In some ways, I knew better, far better than I acted, but in the old life I had not the courage to assert myself. I cannot forgive myself for this neglect."

He seated himself, and bowed his head in deep humiliation.

Then many voices joined in the song
"Work on, work on, the harvest time is coming
    By and by."

"Will Phillips Brooks now honor us with his thoughts upon this subject?"

There was a subdued murmur of admiration expressed by the audience as he arose before them with a majesty and symplicity of bearing that seemed to express the thought before he opened his lips. When he did speak, the first sentence was like an emancipation proclamation! "I would have men free! I would have my church people free from error; for they are in error! I do not mean merely the handful that I ministered to in my dear old home, but I would have every organization which has arisen out of the old Episcopalian faith, free! Like my brother, I see the chains. 'I believe in the resurrection of the body.' *Strike that out!* for thousands of lips say those words and act as though they have no belief in their truth! My body! would I have it again? clumsy and uncouth; could it compare with the one I now have? and this is not yet faultless. Consider the thought, my friends; if a time were ever coming when we would all have to return to those cramped conditions, try to waken the echoes of memory in the old brain, use the old, weary hands; and some of you would have to take that old, wrinkled flesh and rejuvenate it.

Would its yellow hue compare with the transparency of this spiritual flesh with which we are clothed? Could we cause our spiritual blood to flow through the old veins and arteries? Would the old heart respond to such spiritual fluids as we send through these throbbing veins? Would the old nerves awake to new action and do their wonderful work of telegraphing to all parts of the body?

No! no! Lie still pale hands! Your work is done. Grey matter of the brain, get out of your prison wall! and send your strength out into nature's vast store-house—pulseless heart, make the heart of a rose, pink in memory of the faithful service you have given, in sending the red blood to give life to manhood's prime. Old limbs, once so strong, let your bones and sinews give force and strength to trees, whith which to shelter graves where no other monuments are erected in memory of life's battles. Old bodies of generations past, bring up beauty to the world, but not disease.

Yes, this thought has grown upon me more and more. Let us all agree upon this truth.—*There is no resurreetion of the physical body!*"

Then the people sang—

"One step at a time and the hight is reached."

"We will now hear from Mr. Spurgeon, world-renowned, and people of the higher spheres now recognize him as a worker."

Mary looked at me and whispered, "He doesn't look emancipated yet;" and I thought so too, by what he said.

"Brethren, I would not cast a note of sadness into your day of rejoicing; but are you not going too far—very much too far? I cannot approve of this course. I deeply deplore it. You knock the foundations out. You do not give us a brick to stand upon"—

He was here interrupted by Mr. Beecher, who said, "Brother, this meeting is not for discussion, or for comment upon other people's views, but it is for each one to honestly tell what seems to be a mistake in creeds or articles of belief.

What would you have left out of your old faith?"

"Well," said he, very slowly, "I do not care to commit myself except on one point. I would have the idea exploded, that baptism is a saving ordinance. I thought so there, more than I preached it. But since my coming over here I have met several very miserable people who said they had laid so much stress upon baptism that they had neglected other soul requirements, and found an unhappy restlessness about their lives. I would have that stricken out. But I protest"—

Sing—

"Hallelujah, t'is done!"

said Mr. Beecher, before he could say any more.

Rev. John A. Brown was then called upon as a representative of, at first a Presbyterian church and then a Congregational church.

"I was willing to take one step that was a little more liberal while I was there, by stepping into the Congregational church. What would I have stricken out of the old creeds—Foreodination—Election—Infant Damnation, or any danger of it—Sinning away the day of grace: " he hesitated a little, and then said, "the atonement."

"What have you got left?" asked a dozen voices.

"My own individuality," said he, "and a freedom from bondage I never felt before!"

"Tell the glad tidings, another soul is free." rang out on the still air.

Rev. George B. Olney, Unitarian, shouted Mr. Beecher, now thoroughly enthused with the success of the meeting, "What would you have left out of your church ideas?

"Not very much left out, only the pride that keeps our church from wider fields of education. I would have them so strong that when they have a Spiritualist for a minister, they would call him by his right name: not put clogs in the way of those earnest exponents of the idea of communication between two worlds, who are willing to sacrifice for it. 'I get as good Spiritualism as I want, at the Unitarian church,' says one after another, and the moneyed ones flock there because of its popularity, while the real workers for the cause, plod along with little encouragement. I would have real honesty in any religion."

Rev. E. W. Miner, Universalist, said, "I would banish this thought, 'As in Adam all die, so in Christ shall all be made alive;' and give the other thought, that Adam's little affair, if it occurred, could have no influence over us, as it was purely of a domestic nature, and as there can be no death, so we are made alive to all that is beautiful, by strict integrity and a willingness to conquer all things through perseverance, and by doing acts of kindness.

"Sowing seeds of kindness," was the song.

A Methodist divine, whose name I did not catch, was then called upon. He said, Taking the churches all together, he still thought the Methodist church was the best; but there was one practice he objected to, and he was glad to see efforts made to remedy it, and that was the itineracy. He did not like so much moving among pastors.

There was a smile upon the whole audience; and as we had been there some time, Mr. Beecher concluded to dismiss the meeting.

"What an idea!" said Mary, "after all that had been said, that was the only thing he could think of which he would have different! I wish Bishop Haven had spoken. I saw him laughing as though he thought it a huge joke."

I wondered what had been accomplished; and then thought, well, well, that vast audience are the workers, and each one has caught some thought which will be given to those for whom we labor.

S. BOWLES.

PAPER III.

RECEPTION GIVEN TO EMANCIPATORS BY THE EMANCIPATED.

I heard the above announcement but it gave me no special feeling of interest.

"Where is it to be?" inquired my wife.

"At the great Temple," I responded. "It will be a grand meeting if all the Emancipators and Emancipated assemble there. I doubt if there is a building in the upper spheres, large enough to hold them."

"We can go and see," said she. "Oh! what a strange world this is! no cooking, yet we are furnished food—no dress making, yet we are clothed in beautiful garments—no hard toil, only that of the soul, and still all things go on without interruption.

"There is rest for the weary," she hummed.

"Yes, that is so."

We were in time for the reception. What an audience! A pleasant guide met us at one of the many doors and said, "We draw the color line to day. All seats in the main auditorium are reserved for our colored brothers and sisters. You white people can sit in the gallery or in one of the annexes."

"Let us go up stairs," said my wife.

Going up stairs means very little of effort compared to the inconvenience of earthly stairs: so we soon found good seats. As yet there was silence. We beheld thousands of colored people: no talking nor laughing. There was only a look of suppressed excitement and expectation upon their faces. The large platform was empty.

When every seat was taken, an unseen organist touched the keys of the great organ and it responded with such notes of welcome as made the heavens echo to the sound.

"I can think the words which belong to that tune," said Mary, "although perhaps they have never been written. Its all"——

She was interrupted by the coming upon the platform of Harriet Beecher Stowe, leaning upon the arm of Frederick Douglass. They were followed by Abraham Lincoln, John Brown, Lucretia Mott, William Lloyd Garrison, Wendell Phillips, Theodore Parker and numbers of others whose names I must omit for want of space.

Silently, yet simultaneously every man and wo-

man had risen to their feet, and the heads of the colored people were bowed in prayer and silent blessing. Then as with one accord, they sang,
"Blest be the tie that binds
Our hearts in heavenly love.".

Frederick Douglas then arose and in part, said "We are met here to-day to do honor to our emancipators. This acquisition to our number may have inspired the earlier convening of this vast assembly. My brothers and sisters, look upon the face of one whose pen aroused a great nation to thinking in our behalf, and welcome Harriet Beecher Stowe as the leading emancipator of our race.

Without her work, the fire of emancipation would not have so soon been kindled—without her sacrifice of time for writing, the message to the world would never have been given—without her courageous spirit which braved church, state and nation, there would have been long delay in sending forth word pictures of what it was to be a slave. Uncle Tom's Cabin entered the libraries of the rich in crowded cities—it found a place in the farm home —it lay upon the chair of the cottage of the poor— it awakened kings, queens and emperors to the thought of slavery as it found expression in the so called 'land of the free' —it entered the homes of slave owners, and when read, was hidden from view.

'Trouble will come to us from this book,' said hundreds of southern statesman. A premonition of future disaster in consequence of their human chattels seemed to be the prevailing opinion.

Yet redemption was a long time coming. It came at last, in ways we will consider later. Will you say a few words, Mrs. Stowe?"

That noble woman, whom all must honor, simple in her bearing, with her strong, brave and now beautiful face, illuminated with heavenly light, looked up to the higher spheres and said, "Not mine the work, but thine, Oh! heavenly messengers of peace and freedom! My brothers and my sisters, "Uncle Tom's Cabin" was a partnership creation. I gave my time, my fullest sympathy: I made a study of southern scenes and character, and yet I could never have put the spirit into the book which still lives, if I had not been dominated by a superior power. My characters talked for themselves, they dominated me: thank God, these strange evangels have done a portion of the great work.

But had there been none to take up the dropped threads, had there been no Garrison, no Phillips, no Parker, no John Brown, no Lincoln—had there been none of these to light the flame of freedom for the slave, my work would have been unfinished in that direction, when I came over here.

All honor to the multitudes who sacrificed home, friends, life, even, for the fulfillment of the prophesies of thousands of spirits from this realm, and who helped along the cause of our dark-browed brothers and sisters. But I am not here to talk," said she, smiling, "I will let the others of my family do the talking," glancing toward her brothers, who were upon the platform. "I worked more with the pen. I have a loved sister* in earth life, who should talk more," she added in her quiet way, "and I hope she will improve the time left."

Shout after shout of "Bless God, Glory to God," and kindred exclamations were uttered as she took her seat.

---
* Isabella Beecher Hooker.

Frederick Douglas continued, "I would like to tell you something of Mrs. Stowe's entrance into this life. For days we had watched her, even though her earth friends at that time, did not realize how near she might be to this side of life. Had she been fully conscious of it herself, she would have said with the poet—

"I know I am nearing the heavenly ranks
Of friends and kindred dear,
For I brushed the dew on Jordan's banks,
The crossing must be near."

How eagerly we watched her in these last months and up to the time of her coming. How the freedmen and women gathered around, and asked, "Will it be in a few hours or will it be days before she comes to us?"

Though the end was like the ceasing of a leaf to respond to the gentle breath of summer, yet to thousands of these waiting ones of every hue and from every clime, it was a call to duty—to make the first hours of her spirit life here, a revelation of power! Seeing her own dear relatives, passing close around her, and then the multitudes of enfranchised ones waiting in a silence that made silence eloquent, she smiled and said, " Thank God, they do remember me!"

Still, midst our rejoicing, I know there is sorrow in earth life, for it is something to lose from any hearth-stone, from any community, such a strong self-poised character as that of our sister. Yet she was always kind. There was sweetness in every letter she wrote. The kindness with which she treated everybody, made her life a fragrance, and leaving earth life, a personal sorrow to hundreds.

I think that human love always stands, bewildered between its own sense of loss and the glory into which its loved ones have gone.

The power of all appreciation is, I think, largely due to the power for comparison; and if we can only send to the people of earth, our heavenly messages, with such strength as will show them clearly, the difference between the earthly mist and the heavenly glory, I think all will soon learn that mourning is selfishness.

Harriet Beecher Stowe's life here is the life of a worker, who has hardly time for rest. Her brother, Henry said to her, 'Get acquainted with heaven, Harriet, and choose your work later on,' and she is trying to follow his advice."

After a song, I was very much pleased with the course taken. Mr. Douglas said, "Now, friends, brothers and sisters, we do not want great speeches, but honest ones from your lips, and very short ones, we have no time to waste."

No. 1, a colored man rose and said, "My knowin' far suah 'bout her was like gettin ligin fore one's red de Bible. I had my freedom fore I red dat udder Bible for us, cullard fo'ks, 'Uncle Tom's Cabin.' "

No. 2, a colored woman said, "I hav a 'quest to make to de bressed Missus, will she sumwhar in dis hebenly kingdom jes let me tech de finger ob little Miss Eva? I said, suah I'd find her in heben, but I dun cant yit. Bress de Lawd, tho I'se foun yo.' '

No. 3 said, Missy Sto' we's got inter a new place ter see you; neber cum heyar fore, ony wunce, dat time wus ter see Massa Linkum. Are yo' dun suar Uncle Tom is roun heyar sumwhar? I'd like kiss de stripes dat waked de pity in yo' hart an helped ter make us free. An if all de rest ob de wurld had bin no 'count fo'ks, de Lawd would hab made a heben jes fer yo' an Maasa Linkum an Massa Brown an all dem good brudders, I gess."

No. 4 said, "Glory ter Gawd; Uncle Tom's stripes all lef on de ole body, an we got free by anudder's stripes—de good Book sa so. Now, Missy, is it wickud fer us, poor cullurd fo'ks ter wish we find dat ole Lergree an gib him sum stripes? Low, ornary fellar; he 'serves em."

"He has got the stripes, all the Legrees have, my brother," said Mr. Douglas, rising. He then called upon a man with a very black face, who rose and made one of the most impassioned speeches of the day. Others followed in quick succession until Mr. Douglas introduced Abraham Lincoln.

Great shouts of welcome went up. Mr. Lincoln bowed as though not intending to make a speech, and turned to take his seat; but he was not allowed to take it. He was compelled to say a few words. "When the warp and woof of a great fabric is placed in the hands of one holding a sacred trust, could he do aught else than to set the great loom in motion to complete the fabric. That was my position. I turned the wheel which set the machinery in motion. It was with doubts and misgivings, yet the wheels went round. There is no credit due to me, only as one of the spokes in the great wheel of emancipation. 'Uncle Tom's Cabin' was the hub, for it opened eyes and gave power. God bless you all."

John Brown said, his work, looking from his present stand point, was ill advised, but still it was all he knew how to do then. He hoped his work for humanity in other lines of enfranchisement, would be of a more healthy kind.

"Yours was good 'nuff, good 'nuff," shouted the crowd."

Lucretia Mott, on being introduced, said she believed it was her strict sense of justice, which gave her the desire to work in the cause of the slave. "I was not cumbered by creeds, I did not know there was any certainty of life after death of the body, but I concluded, short or long, every creature deserved the best to be obtained from life."

"Theodore Parker said his life could not have been more enthused in any cause than that of the slave, but he still deplored the great sacrifice, which might, he believed, have been avoided.

Wendell Phillips said, "the old doctrine of 'whatever is, is right,' applied to this as well as to any cause—that it was to be. American soil was to receive the blood of the slain, to show that *principle* was above all other interests—that he hoped the time of such dire necessities was past. It is idle to talk about buying those millions of slaves. It could not have been done. A nation's money was not meant to be used to cater to a wrong so deep-dyed as human *slavery!* and thus make a whole nation a party to the thought of buying up immortal beings! To-day every drop of blood, shed for the freedom of a country from this thralldom, is doubly blessed."

Garrison said, people always know how to doctor a patient after the patient is dead. Those who would have freed the slaves without bloodshed, would have been central figures in the world of men and women. I do not like, my brothers and sisters, to think back to slavery, but I rather think of present freedom and future possibilities. Educate them, help them now and let vain regrets be buried in the grave of the past.

Mr. Douglass said, there were many people he would like to call upon, but it would be impossible, as the Temple would soon be used for another and a different gathering. "My heart is full of gladness at this expression of love aud sympathy which has been extended to our Emancipators. It is well known that the purpose of this meetiug is to bring Mrs. Stowe more personally before the public; for she is still working. The Beecher family can't stop; they will find work which will soon make the upper spheres more delightful for their coming; and so should we all be glad."

After a farewell song we went home; Mary saying, regretfully. "I wish I had done something in earth life that would be as well remembered as has been the work of Mrs. Stowe."

"Be content, dear, your work was not without results, and results grow as heaven expands."

"Bless all the workers," said she.

S. BOWLES.

PAPER IV.

An Interview with Jay Gould.

"I am going to see Jay Gould this morning," I said to Mary, " and hear what he will say, now that he has been here long enough to understand the difference between the two realms."

Mary said, "Very likely he wont say anything to you except rail-road bonds and stocks and such things. I cannot imagine how any one, so deeply immersed in money making, can have any intelligent ideas of this spiritual life. I do not think I will go with you."

We can go with almost lightning speed if there is need of it, but heaven would be robbed of its beauty and pleasure if we could not stroll along as we did in the old life, drinking in its beauty, and in that way, from the very fullness of our souls, enjoying that which the Infinite has spread out for our pleasure. Thus when life is overflowing with the rapture of living, we feel what it is to praise God.

I went across the green of a beautiful park. No signs, "Keep off the grass" were there; for we are free to go as we will. Children were playing there, rolling nearly up to a fountain which sent its silver spray out over the grass; then rolling back in a great hurry, to get "out of the wet." The grass bent down under their light bodies, but the recuperative power of all things here is so great, that nothing can be destroyed—the life principle in all things is beyond the hand of the destroyer.

A group of litle folks was gathered around one of the seats upon which was seated a wise little maiden, who was telling a wonderful secret to them. "My Mamma is coming up here. My dear little baby brother came as soon as he was born ; and now Grandma says, Mamma is coming to take care of the baby : and I must be real good to her, so she wont worry about Papa and brother Henry. I shouldn't think she would do that. Great big men can take care of themselves, and Henry is most as tall as Papa."

"I've got a nice little verse which I am practicing on. I made it all myself; and I think its beautiful : and I am speaking it to Mamma every time they let me go to her : but she don't hear me yet. When she gets her new ears she will hear me. Its this ;" and the sweet voice of the child sounded loud and musical in the clear air;—

"Dear Mamma, come to my home with me,
    You are tired of waiting, I know,
And baby, he needs you so awfully bad,
    For Grandma, she says it is so.
Dont you think that is pretty?"

"Yes, yes," said several voices, but one thoughtful girl timidly suggested that she thought some other word in a poem from heaven, than 'awfully' would sound better."

"Well, I can't help it, when it sounds just true to me, and Mamma will know what it means : I think it is just as well," said the decided little Miss. "You are so 'ticular, I guess you was 'bornded' in heaven."

"No, I wa'nt either, but I like things nice."

So you see that children here have their differences in opinion as well as in earth life.

Further along, I saw a group of young women-students in Botany.

"I cannot recall what family this flower belongs to," said one girl, puckering up her brows in her effort to think. She held in her hand a rare specimen whose name I did not know even after quite a sojourn here.

"You will find as I have found, child," said a grave-looking woman, who had joined the group, "that earthly Botany will not fit heavenly flowers. Become familiar with our higher lessons and a heaven of beauty will open unto you."

Still farther on, a sour-visaged man joined a group of men who were discussing some pleasant subject, evidently by their looks, and asked, "Can you direct me to a place where I can enter a complaint? I have been kept awake by loud singing and it is an infringement on the rights of another for such conduct to be allowed. I have not seen a policeman since my arrival."

"The few policemen here, wear citizen's clothes," was the answer, "and they may be among the singers who disturbed you."

Another of the party took the hand of the puzzled man and said, "You have come to a land of song and rejoicing. Strive to attune your heart to this music, which falls upon my ears like a benediction from the Infinite."

Grumbling in Heaven, I mused as I passed along.

I soon reached the home of Jay Gould, and found him willing to receive me. Everything in his surroundings, was simple, yet beautiful.

When he learned the purport of my visit, he said, "Do you think they really do get the knowledge you try to impart to them? Do they of earth really believe it? I have tried so often to communicate to my own children, but my own doubt and their lack of knowledge upon these questions, have blocked the way and I do not know how much ready-found room is in their hearts."

"Will you tell the story of your life since you came here?" I asked.

"Oh! no, I cannot: it would take too many chapters of your book. I will just give you a glimpse of my life here. I had no really substantial views of what this life would be before I came. I was so hurried, I had no time for study upon this subject. I wanted to accumulate property. It became a mania with me, so I came over here like a child, with all of my wealth left behind. And when the little step from that life to this was taken, when I awoke to the full knowledge that I was really what the world calls dead, I was surprised, yet in a way, pained. My desires carried me back to the earth. I wanted to see how affairs were getting on. I saw in my will that which I wanted changed, for I had no moral right to put one child in the power of the other children. I saw things neglected which needed attention, but I could not make them hear one word of advice.

At last a longing desire came to me to know what the world said of me, and I listened to some of the notices as read from earthly papers. They all spoke of my wonderful business qualifications—of my extreme good fortune in turning everything into money—of how rich I had left my children, but not any thought of what good I had tried to do. Mr. Bowles, I was hurt a little, for I was not all selfishness. I had never heralded my gifts: I had rather told the recipients to say nothing about their gifts. I had not given largely to religious organizations, for I had not much sympathy for them, but if you look around this upper country, you will see those who will bless Jay Gould for what he did for them, and in earth life I can point to homes that I helped to build for the poor. I do not say this in praise of myself, only in justification of myself. I would not want the world to believe that the fountain of goodness was entirely dried up in my nature, for it was not so. But I can see now where I erred: I did not enter enough into the spirit of reform and charity. While preoccupied with other subjects which seemed of such great importance, I did not stop to study into public needs and public questons, save as they related to finance, and thus I crippled my soul. I can raise my voice with you, Mr. Bowles, against monopolies. I see the bearing they have upon the world at large. Oh! if men could only know how to get rich in a way that riches would last, I should be glad. When I first came here, I was so eager to learn. I wanted to go back to earth life, and when I was attracted to scenes which harrowed my heart, or listened to stories of wretchedness such as I never dreamed existed, I would raise my voice and say, 'I will give,' but when I would name the sum, I found I had nothing to give—empty pockets—I went over the old ground from New York to Missouri. I looked at agents who had been long in my employ. I tried to impress them with their carelessness, but they would not listen.

I went to my own. I saw sorrow there, but still I could not at that time reach them so that they would in the least fulfil even mechanically my desires.

But as the years have passed, a band of us have touched the brain of one of my children and we have helped to make her life beautiful in the extreme: and I know, Mr. Bowles, she is doing good. Her heart is beating for humanity. Her work is so well chosen and effective. 'My precious Helen,' he continued, musingly, 'what may I not hope from you!' And then I will reach the others: Oh! they do not realize the life of sacrifice I lived to accumulate that money which is going out of their hands so easily. They do not know the power from this side which was felt by me. I did not know it then, but now I find I had those about me whose accumulating spirit made me think far more of wealth than I otherwise should. As I think it over now, I see that at times, instead of the money, it was more a desire to keep things moving—to turn the key of business life and see its vast machinery set in motion—to feel the heart beats of the great mass of men who worked from early morn till weary night to bring in something for me.

Oh! that life was full of varying moods, but still surrounding all was a dogged determination to conquer fate—to stand at the head of the world of finance—to wield supreme power in that realm.

How worse than idle were my ambitions? The Reaper came before the grain was ripe, and with my life unripened by the holiest of earthly experiences, I am here to finish up."

"How do you spend your time?"

"Well, much of it with Helen. I can reach her best. I hope to do by proxy what I never did myself. And then with my boys—I want to watch yet about the leaks," he said, with a twinkle in his eye. "I hav'nt got over that yet. I also go around among my old friends and try to wake them up; but sometimes I fail of even making them think of me. I am trying to put the commercial part of life away from me, but its hard work.

I aim to reach earth life now from a soul standpoint. That is hard work too; bnt I shall work my way along.

Helen was very much impressed by Moody's sermons. I hope she wont get into that rut. Where am I if what he says is true?

Well I thank you for coming, but I have an appointment at this time in the the city."

"Business," I asked.

"Forgive me," he said, "and stay as long as you can. It was the force of habit that made me say that."

I soon said good by, and went home. I told my wife all about it. and she said, "Oh! how mistaken we can be in mortals?

S. BOWLES.

PAPER V.

OBSTACLES TO THE DEVELOPMENT OF THE INHABITANTS OF THIS LIFE OF THE SPIRIT.

"What are you going to write about now, Samuel," said Mary as she closely watched my method of controlling this medium.

"Can't you see what I have written as a heading, Mary?"

"No, I can't, I expect I never shall be very wise. I see some things I do not want to see, and now, when I see by this wonderfully strange process, that you are effecting the hand so it will write in the old world, I can only see the dark marks but not the words."

She has gone away now, fearing she will disturb me. If you of that life knew how hard it is to give you intelligent thought, how many of our processes for its transmission are the result of years of careful study by our best scientific spirits, you would be less harsh in your judgment.

Our thoughts which we would impart are often so emasculated in the transmission, that they become as trivial as those of an unlettered tyro in comparison to those of the careful student. Our pictures, painted by the hand of an unseen artist touching the hand of an earthly artist, are in comparison to our work in this sphere like the wood cuts of a third-class newspaper, to the careful creation of an artist who has studied long years in sunny Italy and drawn inspiration from the grandeur of the Alps.

I have recently met a Mrs. Blair who used to paint flower pieces while in earth life, when blindfolded, and that too with only one hand. The colors were placed separately upon her palette, yet she always selected or made the right shades, and did work which was called marvellous, and so it was in the way it was done.

"How do you feel about your work since you have come to this side?"

"Disappointed," said she, "though I do not like to say it, I have said it to the one who was my faithful guide, and we quite agree now: but at first it was hard for my guide to understand that what I had left behind was not true art. She had great power over my hand in selection of colors and never made a mistake; yet the groupings were wrong and the shading often very imperfect. But that was not the worst defect: there were but few leaves or buds, right in their proportions—the most of them being too wide for the length, and thus the whole picture looked inharmonious.

Had my guide educated herself in art, or at least accepted the opportunity offered to advance to a higher degree of skill before using her power to control, it would have been much better. I regret to say that even now, although she acknowledges her imperfection, she is developing another medium in earth life to give to the world the same kind of defective work, and in that way, continue to increase the impression that the denizens of this life are not advancing as is claimed by the exponents of truth in earth life."

IMMATURE MEDIUMSHIP.

"What do you consider to be the most serious consequences resulting from the public exercise of immature mediumship."

"It is a great impediment to the progress of the individual spirit here. The people of earth will get over the shock at the inartistic work, and will say 'that's more of human work than of spiritual,' but the guide who is striving to be a teacher when she herself is untaught, will miss for a long time the joy of a true artist of the spirit realm."

'Are you satisfied with none of the work done?"

"Well, there are a few I have seen with my spiritual eyes which have some merit, but very few. I may not have noticed them all. They are in every state and beyond the far seas.

But now I want to know Art. I have two hands now and am learning the fairy touch the Masters teach. Come to our studio, Mr. Bowles, bring your wife and see the pictures from the hands of true artists. It is the large, low building on Magnolia Avenue."

I pondered somewhat whether my desire to greet the earth world with imperfectly expressed thoughts might not be classed as an obstacle to my rapid development. "An honest man must criticise himself" said I; but nevertheless my zeal leads me still farther on, even in an imperfect way.

Then I began a further search for the obstacles to development in spirit life, and found that the root of it all had begun in earth life.

THE TWO BROTHERS.

I had for a long while been attracted to a sad looking man, who seldom spoke to any one, always seeming to be in a deep study. "My friend," I said to him, one morning, "I never see you around among the investigators after truths in this life. May I ask where you find your purest enjoyment?"

"I do not find much that deserves even the name of enjoyment," replied he. "I have never sought to rise. My work has been on the earth plane, and miserable work it has been, too," continued he.

"Will you tell me your story?"

A look of cunning came into his eyes, and he said, "What will you do if I tell it to you?"

"I'll do you no harm, and it may help others," I responded.

"Well," said he, "as they count time on earth, I have been in this life about seventy five years. When I passed away from earth, there was mourning. I was rich, and tried to be good to the tenantry in my possession. The world said I was fortunate to inherit the fortune which should have gone to my brother, but that brother was accused of murder. He would have been hung if he had not escaped from prison, (I knew how) and fled to America. I soon came into possession of my estates by the transition of my father, and I sent my brother, under an assumed name, money to help him along. He was a coward, poor boy, all the way through. His wife married under an assumed name;

his children were born under a wrong name, and this wrong name is now an honored one in the great state of New York, U. S. A.

That which gnawed at my heart there and shadowed me—that which is making of me a haunting shadow in the earth life, is this : I could have given positive proof that my brother was innocent, for I knew it. He did not know that I knew it. It would have brought out before the public, an early indiscretion of mine, if I had told, and I reasoned in this way. 'I am better fitted for the position than is my brother. I can dignify it. I will support him. He shall fare well, (but he did not) and it is best as it is.'

He mourned my passing out as the last link in the chain which connected him with his old life in England, and went on, meekly mute, through daily toil until release came to him. When I saw the end was near, I was with him. Mother and father were there too, and a beautiful sister who passed to spirit life in infancy.

Mother's eyes seemed to reprove me and to say You here! here by your wronged brother's deathbed! and my beautiful sister touched me pityingly.

At last, he came. He saw me first.

" I knew you would meet meet me, brother ; you have been so kind to your forsaken brother. I'm glad you meet me."

He then recognized the rest of the family, and said, "Is there room for an innocent man to stand straight here?"

I said, "Yes, brother, yes,"

"He turned and looked into my soul! My guilt showed in my face.

"Oh! can it be you knew, George and wronged me all these years? Say you did not, I cannot bear it."

He cannot say he might not have prevented all your suffering, Charles. He is guilty, very guilty and does not desire to rise above it," said one.

Then mother said, "Don't say that; you know how hard he is trying to correct the wrong."

"What have his efforts been? merely as 'straws in the wind,'—that is all."

After that they came to me with my wife and children and begged of me to give up this vain effort to enlighten those who do not know that their ancestors were defrauded—to inform them if possible how to obtain that which should have been theirs—or more hopeless still, to attempt to inspire my descendents to give up the property which never really belonged to them.

"Are you not going to adopt the advice of your friends?" I asked.

He shook his head and said, "Not yet. There are some new mediums developing in earth life, whom I must watch. I may be able to control one of them and give evidence."

When I thought of this obstacle to the development of this poor brother, I wondered if it might not be one of the hindrances to the right understanding of spiritual truths. Then I thought how those connected with different branches of the family (for he says it is now large) might receive messages from this side, informing them that they were heirs to property in England, and thus awaken a desire for wealth, only to be disappointed upon inquiry. I've wondered how long this impractical idea would dominate him.

All those whom he directly wronged are now in spirit life, and have forgiven him, but he cannot forgive himself. *This is slow Hell!* I thought as I bade him good bye.

Another obstacle I find to the rapid development of the spirit, is

"KNOWLEDGE IN ONE LINE IN EARTH LIFE TAKEN AS THE ONLY CRITERION OF KNOWLEDGE HERE."

In my rambles, I have met a great student of the law, who talks about it to men, women and children—who says, "I was called proficient in earth life. What would my colleagues think of me, now that I have mastered the difficulties which besieged me there?"

"What are you doing with your knowledge?" I asked him, after he had refused to become interested in any of the beauties of spirit life, or to respond to any of the needs of earth life.

Oh! I'm storing up, storing up, all of the time. I don't intend any one to get ahead of me."

He could not give me any intelligent answer as to his plans. He did not desire to use his gift of great wisdom, on earth, and there were no law suits in heaven. The quandary is, how many hundred years will he continue to be true to his 'calling.'

"Let him alone," said my wife, "Law is his heaven, and all the heaven he wants."

But my opinion is, that study and ambition had burdened his brain there, and his thought during his life here had not rebounded from the pressure.

I might write indefinitely of obstacles to development in spirit life. Those given above are comparatively innocent beside the terrible ones, which have come under my observation. For there are stories as cruel as the grave, to an undisciplined soul, which meet me on every hand. I do not fully understand the import of all of them, but I understand enough to make me desire to speak in thunder tones to those who are in earth life, to lay down all idols, for you will find them to be clay. Break all conditions of habit, whether of body or mind which will serve as a hindrance to rapid progress in spirit life.

S. Bowles.

PAPER VI.

Interesting Scenes Witnessed at Spirit Birth.

My wife said to me one day, as we were looking out upon varied scenery from the porch of our home, "Samuel, can people grow selfish in heaven?"

I was startled by her question, and answered, "Why, no, how can they?"

"I'll tell you," continued she. "To you and me and millions of others, the question is settled. We cannot die. The law is understood; but there are this instant, thousands of people, dying as the world calls it, and we don't go to any of them, to watch and help if we can. Henry* says he finds it one of the sweetest labors he can perform, to be a real helper to the arisen spirits, and in the death scenes too, he says he has made great changes in the feelings of the mourners, and helped to quiet the grief that is so frequent in bereavements. He has made a study of it.

*Henry Alexander, a brother-in law of Mr. Bowles.

Don't you think, Samuel, that we could spare some time and learn how it is done and then devote part of our time to the work. Who knows who next of those we love will come over, and we want to reach them with no uncertain help."

Well, women on both sides of the line of the two worlds are famous for changing man's plans. I was at that time greatly interested in the issue, pending in your Republic there. I was watching the pulse beats of politics, trying to feel that corruption was now a myth, and that statesmanship had reached a much higher condition since my transition; but I listened to her words and said, "Yes, I suppose I can go, but such scenes have always been very distasteful to me, Mary, and I do not know that we can do any good."

"We will do good," replied she; "we will help those whom they know and love to come nearer to them, so they will not feel so much alone."

"Just then Henry called in and said, "There is a young mother to whom I have been attracted who will soon need some one to comfort her. She is one of the bread-winners of life. Her husband is in a drunken sleep; she has given an overdose of some vile compound to her child to keep it asleep, while she goes on with the washing."

TRANSITION OF A CHILD.

As quickly as thought, almost, we were there. Oh! what a home it was! One room and a bed room; but although the washing was being done in one corner, everything about the poorly furnished room was very clean. The table was set for three. At one place was a little plate with a spoon on it, a tin cup at the side and a high chair drawn up to the table. The other two plates were for the drunken husband when he should wake up and for the weary wife.

In the bedroom on a poor bed, was the drunken man. We looked at him with a strange fascination, the high, broad forehead, the clustering brown curls, and then the lower part of the face, giving a lie to the upper part—for it was bloated and disfigured by drink. The hands were delicate and looked unused to hard work. An open account book with amounts partly figured up, showed he had last tried to do something for a butcher in straightening out his accounts.

Henry was beside the child—a golden-haired little one, possibly two and one-half years old. "She is sinking fast! O, can't you influence that mother to come here? Mary went to her, and her voice sounded shrill to me as she implored the mother to come to the child. At last, as though startled by some sound, the mother wiped her hands on her apron and tip-toed into the bed room. Bending low over the crib to kiss her child, she noticed the strange pallor, the quick, short breathing, and she perceived there was danger for her child.

"George! George!" called she; "get up! Nellie's dying, Nellie's dying! and she shook him vigorously.

"Le'me be," said he; but by persevering, she at last awakened him.

"What's the matter, can't you let me sleep. I've got the headache."

"Oh! George, baby's dying! I know she is. Get a doctor, do."

Thoroughly awakened now, he started for the doctor, and though he lived near, the mother was destined to be alone with her dying child.

Oh! the heart aches and the agony expressed by that young mother! "Oh! I've killed my baby! I know I have, I know I have!"

The eyelids quivered and lifted for an instant, but oh! the wonder expressed in them, as the child saw the waiting friends, and a smile as sweet as the the rosy dawn beamed over her face and rested there after the frozen silence of death had placed his seal.

"Take this child," said Henry to a woman who, though a dweller in spirit life, still wore her look of pride, "take this child; it is your duty: she will help you in heaven."

At first, the grandmother rebelled and said, "How can I do it? This child is the fruit of disobedience. I told my daughter, her marriage would separate us on earth and in heaven; and here I am, holding close to my heart, the child of that debauched specimen of humanity." "It is your daughter's child," said Henry; "the same blood runs in its veins as did in yours. It is a part of your life. It will comfort you and make peace between you and your lonely child on earth."

The little child was constantly trying to reach her mother, crying out in sharp, childish accents, striving to get the body which had been hers, out of her mother's arms so she could take its place.

The husband and the doctor had now returned. In cold tones, the doctor inquired, "What did you give the child."

"Some of this," said the mother. "We took it years ago for bowel trouble and baby had not slept any, so I thought I could check the trouble and make her sleep too."

"You have given a double dose," said the doctor, when she told how much she had given.

"No, no, its the same amount they gave my little brother, and it helped him. I distinctly remember it, for I gave him the medicine myself and that was years ago."

"The medicine has dried down to twice its old strength. I hardly know how to make out the certificate of death," mused the doctor, as he passed out.

Neighbors were called in and the now sobered man was trying to aid all he could about the house, and the distracted mother was looking through the scanty wardrobe of the child to find something to clothe the body, when we left.

"Where is the child, now," I asked, as grandmother and child had disappeared.

"The child will do its work, " said Henry: "she is now surprising that cold, proud woman, by making her feel she has not entirely left her daughter out of her life."

"But was it fair to allow that child to be sacrificed to reconcile any one? Is it right."

"I do not know" said Henry, "but I do know the result will be for the betterment of all."

When we went home, we talked it over, but could come to no conclusion.

TRANSITION OF THE ITALIAN. A TOUCHING SCENE.

Some days after, Henry again desired us to visit a death bed scene. What a touching scene! The faithful little woman, who was bustling around to get together their few belongings to pack up, would still keep casting her fond eyes toward her husband, who was reclining on a bedstead, over the slats of which was thrown an old blanket.

"Rest all you can, sleep if you can—the dray will take you with the boxes to the depot and then beloved, we will start for Italy: and when you are there, the soft sea air will work wonders, and you will smell the grapes in the vineyards and see your mother and the children, and we will go to our own little children's graves and make the flowers grow again. We will never leave Italy again, when we get there, will we?"

"Italy never changes," said the sick man "but I feel so strangely, that the journey will be so quick."

"And so it will, my darling, for the good ship will not crawl like the one we came over in. It will go as though it had wings and we hardly know we have started, when we will be there."

The poor soul did not understand that his voyage would be quick, or what was this strange restlessness of her husband, which preceded dissolution. She was untaught in everything save the logic of obedience and the philosophy of patience.

"We will talk all the English we can, and teach them how to talk it, when we get home, won't we?"

"When we get home," echoed the dying man. "Beyond the mountains and the sea, Italy." murmured the man.

The woman went up to him to change the old shawl under his head, that he might rest more comfortably. But the face she touched was wet with the dews of death. Without "wings or footfall" he had reached Italy, which lieth beyond the "Alpine highths of great pain."

"Did you see the children bearing him away?"

"Yes, beautiful, beautiful children!"

"Where did he go?" said Mary.

"To Italy," said Henry, "it will be his home for a little while."

"Our work is with the bereaved one," said Henry; and then, gently as a mother sooths her child to sleep, he helped her spirit friends, who talked in a foreign language, to calm the bereaved one.

"Oh! he said this morning twice, he would soon be well, and I have worked so hard to get him home."

"Did you not know that people never get well of consumption, when it has gone as far as in his case?" asked a kindly neighbor.

"No! no! no! Did you know he must die and never tell one word?" said she.

It was sometime before she would consent to bury the body on this side of the Atlantic; and when she did consent, she said, "The last words he said were about Italy. I'll go there to meet him."

"Poor soul," said Mary; "how much of sorrow there is in that beautiful world: but I do wish to find that spirit, sometime, who preferred Italy to heaven.

Transition of a Church Devotee.

The next visit was to a woman, well known in church and in religious circles, who was passing out.

"She cannot need us," Mary said, "for hers was a life so strict that no one around dare utter a worldly sentence."

"We will be beside her just the same, at the request of her daughter in spirit life."

The low voice of the kneeling clergyman sounded deep and solemn through the still room. "Though I walk through the valley of the shadow of death, I will fear no evil, for Thou art with me, Thy rod and Thy staff, they comfort me," and "There shall be no night there."

"No night," echoed the dying woman, "but its dark now. Why does not my Savior appear?"

Her eyes were wide open, trying to see. "Oh no! no! there's people here, those I know, some of our folks. Oh! it must be a delusion! a delusion! I am looking for the Divine face. Come to me, oh! 'Thou who died for me.' The clock ticks so loud I cannot hear His voice. Oh! take the delusion away from me, Oh! Lord! Do not let me be deluded at the last! I think I see my daughter!"

"Quiet your mother," said Henry to the girl. "Now speak, her spirit ears are opened."

"Mother, it is I," said the girl distinctly.

"It is my child!" The lips parted in a smile. One moment with the child she knew, had conquered the prejudices of years.

Mary and I were strongly affected by this scene. "Can we learn to do that?" said Mary. "Can I make my own see me when they are coming over?"

"We will try," I answered.

Later on we saw that mother and daughter. The mother was still calling for the sights she had been taught to expect—for the golden streets and God upon His throne. "I am not in Heaven," said she. "After all, I fear I have not been redeemed. Am I among the saved?" said she, pleadingly. "It is so human here. I cannot believe it is well with my soul."

Henry accompanied us for a few moments and said, "Such cases as the one you have last witnessed are very frequent. Sometimes I think that the Cause which opens the eyes of the people of earth to the fact of the naturalness of heaven, must be moving very slowly, when I witness such numbers of transitions as that of the one just liberated from the body. It is pitiful in the extreme. They have educated themselves away from all that is homelike or beautiful. They have made their lives a sort of martyrdom there, denying the flesh, and placing all human ties under their feet, if in any way they hinder the ideal life of sanctification, only to wake up here to learn that the purest heavenly bliss is won by keeping the ties of nature sacred and through that love, learning to behold nature's God."

"How Henry has progressed!" said Mary. "I cannot understand some of the lessons he would teach us."

"And he is only on the threshold of knowledge," I said."

"We will all learn more in a few millions years," said she, smiling.

S. BOWLES.

PAPER VII.

ONE OF THE WEIGHTS WHICH MENACE OUR NATION.

"While in earth life I dealt less with the religions of the day, than I did with current politics. But looking from this side, with the clearer sight of spirit life, I am emphatic in saying that the most harmful monopoly in the United States is the monopoly of the Roman Catholic Church! We know this church is the oldest Christian church extant—that from it has emerged people of other faiths or slightly changed ones, who are in turn, putting their wares upon the world as from the original package, as the fountain source of Truth.

If I remember history rightly, it was in the fourth century of the Christian era that the Latin or Roman Catholic church assumed authority over the other Churches. Iræneus, Tertullian, Clement of Alexandria and other church fathers corrupted the religion of Papias and others, and from their own devices and ingenuity, built up the church of Rome.

A few of the questions and answers in their Catechism are in themselves enough to show the world, what a power, entirely man-made, is resting over its adherents.

* " How are we known to be Christians ?"

"By being baptized, by professing the doctrines of Christ."

---

* As I am quoting from memory, the language may not be correct. but the spirit is preserved. Some of the questions are asked at the confessional.

How easy the road! The child is baptized in infancy. At the age of twelve to fourteen, it is confirmed in the Church of Rome, learns how much he or she owes to the Church, confesses and is safe. From that age, the child learns secrecy, hypocrisy, and is urged to get money for the church.

The sin of commission may be forgiven by the priest, but the sin of omission is much harder to forgive.

"Have you neglected in any way to bring gifts for the Church of our Lady, which you might have given?" is often asked; and if the culprit has actually given money to others, even to relations, or neglected to drive a sharp bargain, there are numerous ways of punishment, all of which mean self-denial, often in the extreme.

"By professing the doctrine of Christ," and by the "Sign of the Cross." "By professing Christ." Wisely said, for it is professing, not possessing the attributes of the Nazarine. "By the sign of the Cross." Oh! cruel mockery which brings the Ideal of many to the gutter—to the murderer's chamber, where the innocent fruits of their unholy lives are baptized, then strangled out of existence, while their heads are yet wet with baptismal water, and the bystanders unite in giving the "Sign of the Cross."

"Where are true Christians to be found?"

"In the true Church."

"What do you mean by the true Church?"

"The congregation of the faithful, who being baptized, partake of the same sacraments, profess the same doctrines and are governed by their lawful pastors, under one visible head on earth."

"What do you call the true Church?"

"The Holy Catholic Church."

"Is there any other true Church beside this?"

"No, there is but one true Church."

"Are all obliged to be of the true Church?"

"Yes, he that believeth shall not be condemned."

This claim that no one else has the least right to consider himself or herself a Christian, has obtained since the time of Constantine.

Sometime, I believe, in the ninth century, dissention arose during the reign of the emperor, Michael which, two hundred years later, resulted in a division. The Latin Church declared that the Holy Ghost proceeded from the Father and the Son, while the Greek Church declared that it proceeded from the Father alone.

As the centuries passed, the sixteenth century marked a new era in science and letters, and even in religion; yet the Church of Rome sank lower still in vice and crime.

At this time, Leo X was Pope of Rome. But "Fate is not always upon a throne, or in a papal chair." At that time two minds were destined to shape future events, one was that of a young monk in a convent in Germany; the other, a gay Spanish soldier behind the walls of Pampeluna.

The crowned heads at that time, young and full of passion, demanding of life more than its full measure, had little time to spare for the affairs of the Church, and Pope Leo was not living as a holy father of the Church, but as a debased man with all the wealth he could command to carry on his corrupt practices.

He did not know that in this German convent was a man who would be known through the centuries as one who revolutionized ideas to such an extent that it was made possible for almost any new idea to take root with the people. At that time Ignatius Loyola, the soldier dropped his guitar, and ceased singing sweet songs to Spanish lasses, and began to study into the power of mind over mind. He established the "Order of the Jesuits" which linked together a strong chain in another direction, a chain, which though weakened has never been broken.

Martin Luther, after long and earnest prayer, after days of fasting, after strong denunciations had been heaped upon him by his companions and superiors, denounced the sale of indulgences and "burned the bull," which Pope Leo had issued against him for the same.

It was an act which will live in the hearts of the lovers of freedom as long as the word Freedom has a meaning. It touched the hearts of the multitude with fear and wonder, and then with admiration.

Pope Leo tried by ridicule and apparent indifference, to turn the minds of the people from the daring act, while Henry the VIII, came to his rescue and strove to make his influence count for the distressed Pope.

All was of no avail. The conflagration had started on his way. It must light up the minds of the people.

Luther had made a move in a new direction, but he had only exchanged the Pope for the Bible. He had gained a step, one that will make his name immortal ; but it has since been hard to understand which was the real doctrine of Jesus, the one he taught, or the one he rejected.

With this history of the past before me, with the needs of the earth world apparent, with the spiritual light shining into my life, irradiating my pathway with a splendor which no pen can describe. I am looking at you there, almost unconscious of the power of the Church of Rome. She has been shaken, but to stand more firmly. Disturbed on one continent, only to plant her fangs more strongly into the body of a young Republic. Antagonized, only to conquer at last, and to be embraced in the sheltering arms of a great nation.

We from this side are saying, "What do they mean to do? they who act so listless, with an enemy at their doors."

And we answer our own question with another, and say, "What can they do?"

Catholicism, with its subtle force will yet rule the land, if the people do not awake to a sense of duty. Already the press has largely been won over by the power of that church ; the politicians, by its force of numbers—those in fashion's realm by the glare and glitter and beauty of its wonderful architecture and master pieces of art—the poor, by its extensive charities.

Where is there a chance for American men in an American nation!

The Catholic police jostles the honest man in his search for work, if he pause for a few moments to look at displayed comfort, he cannot hope to own.

The carriages or repositories for the proceeds of extensive begging excursions, labeled "The Little Sisters of the Poor, " block the way so the honest cartman cannot deliver his load on time; and thus is despoiled of part of his earnings.

The public school system has, in many instances bowed to its power. Demands have been made in many states for public moneys for parochial schools. Children are being taught in the arts of war as much as in the arts of peace. Honored positions are given the American citizen who is a Catholic, which would be withheld with a feeling that it was just, from a Free Thinker or Spiritualist, on account of belief or non-belief.

All these events are transpiring every day, and you as a people are not setting your forces in a new direction for liberty.

Rome has stained her paths with blood! Do you want more blood? Rome has slaughtered her innocents! Do you want more slaughter? Rome has her heel upon the American nation—her iron heel! and you there are treating it as a child's toy!

S. Bowles.

PAPER VIII.
Mental Therapeutics.

I have been for years deeply interested in those phases of belief which have come from our life to yours, sometimes much misunderstood; yet still retaining some of the elements which spirit workers intended them to retain, although misnamed and wrongly taught. Yet the basic principle was there, whether under the name of Christian Science or under the name of Mental Science, Faith Cure or any other name.

Under all these names, the science of Mental Therapeutics remains the same; and I am much gratified that at last, physicians are waking up to the matter enough to recognize the soul as well as the body, in the patients intrusted to their care; and that in one school, (the Homeopathic) there is an effort being made to more thoroughly understand mental conditions, so as to tune up lumps of clay to go on doing good service.

The intricate machinery of the human form is a house with a man or a woman inside of it; and like some very poor housekeepers, there are many who do not know how to keep house; and the dispatches sent along the nerves of the stomach to the brain, are of a most trying character.

Could I again dwell in an earthly body, I know how to pay it greater respect, by keeping the soul in tune, and remembering that the first ailment which comes, must be a shock to some set of nerves, which telegraphs to the brain, "This man is sick;" and it may be, though the disturbance is slight at first, the wires get down around the liver, and cause inaction, get tangled up around the heart and cause palpitation, touch the small and large veins and cause pressure of blood upon the brain, until the conditions become such that the tenant has little or no control of his house.

The old school physician begins at once upon the body. He wants to clean out the house by force, and so drugs are brought into requisition. Even if they have the desired effect, they help to sever the relations between a man and the house he lives in. After such heroic treatment, he does not restore the message department for a long time; because so many wires are down between body and soul. Though the house may look better, there is a lack in mental power and also a lack of control of the body.

Of course he keeps on thinking, but thought force, when not discriminately used, may be destructive instead of constructive.

Mental Therapeutics, when well understood, will prevent the wear and tear of the house. The ablest physicians will soon see that they must educate themselves in another department—that these drugs are forces which are working against nature, and that success is only to be brought about by an understanding of the partnership of soul and body.

It was my privilege to attend a pleasant party, where several physicians had met to discuss Mental Therapeutics. It was an informal party, and being a friend of one of the physicians, I was welcomed to their midst. They were asked to relate their experiences when in earth life, in some one case, where they had been successful in healing by will or soul power. I will report a few of the instances, which to me were most interesting.

A veteran physician said, "I was for years a Materialist. I have often grieved my gentle wife by saying, 'I have dissected many a body and found a meaning in every nerve, cord, membrane and tissue, have known what each bone and sinew meant, and the part they had to play, but I never found a hole for a soul, and I don't believe there is any soul.' But my gentle wife dropped by my side one day, and somehow I wanted something of her to love.

I tried to study into spiritualistic ideas, but was unfortunate in my experiences. At last I began to study in a scientific way into the relations between the body which is moved and the power which moves it—the brain which thinks and the power which makes it think. Indeed I was in search of a living, compelling force, which dominates the human structure—this wonderful, subtle something called "Life," chained my attention. I wanted to know what became of the "Life," after it had moved from the old house; and I wanted still more to know how it could be made to think away pain— in short, whether the mental went on living or not. I desired to see the effort of combined mental force upon disease.

About that time, a young woman whom I had known from her babyhood, came to me in great distress. She had tried not to believe it, but now she knew from late irritation, she had a cancer on her breast. Her mother had died with a cancer and it was in the blood as far back as she knew anything of her family, on her mother's side. I examined it, and found that although it made little show upon the surface, there was a deep-seated tumorous condition, quite alarming.

I was truthful in confirming her fears, but untruthful in what I afterwards said. "Why, don't you know we have now a positive cure for all cancers at the stage yours is now in?"

"No," she said, brightening up, "I thought nothing but the knife would help, and often that was useless."

Said I, "I will come over toward nightfall with what you will have to use, and give you full directions."

I mused thus, That woman has a cancer all too far developed, and her belief in its fatality will make it fatal. Otherwise, she has a good physique. It will do no harm to see if the combination of two mental forces will drive out disease.

I put some salt and water in a bottle and labelled it, "Poison," and called on my patient. I gave the strictest orders that the bottle should be kept under lock and key, when not in use—to put a few drops in some water. I told her to put a compress upon her breast every night and to wet the cloth two or three times during the night, but to invariably burn the cloths, and to wash and rinse her hands after each application.

"You believe in killing out one poison with a more deadly one, do you not, doctor?"

I, poor sinner, answered in the affirmative.

"I am better already," said she, two days after. "I do not feel the itching or the stinging pain which I have felt and had felt for weeks before anything showed on the outside."

I told her I was glad, that I knew it would cure her—that she must know it too; and as she looked me straight in the eye, she said, "I do know it, doctor."

Her knowing it and my knowing it, helped more than the salt and water. In the course of three weeks there was not the least cancerous symptom about her.

"What did you give her to throw off the poison from her system?" asked one of the doctors.

"Nothing. Nature did her work; and two minds against one cancer was too much for it. Now that I know of the spiritual battery which was brought to bear, I know the hosts of heaven were against it too."

Another of the physicians told of experiments with cases of obstinate hysterics. Another, of a condition which assumed typhoid fever from having been exposed and the belief that she had the disease.

Another told of a consumptive patient, with all the general symptoms, characteristic of the belief in his predisposition to it and many other cases were cited which showed plainly that the knowledge of the spirit world will mingle with that of the earth world until Mental Therapeutics has become the physician to health ose under its care.

So I will hail with delight as will others of this life, the grand era when the power of the soul shall be recognized as superior to the wasting tissues of the body, or at least until the worn-out casket must like a chrysalis, burst its shell for the ripened spirit to enter upon new experiences. Scientific men and women here, say there is no reason why souls should not dwell in their material bodies for a hundred years. Personally, I have no desire to stay so long, but many cling to earth.

S. Bowles.

PAPER IX.

Mental Therapeutics. (Concluded.)

This subject has a strong fascination to me, and from this side where we can see the spiritual anatomy, where we can see the wheels go round, it seems possible to make the tenant far superior to the home he lives in.

The world has always had its born leaders and always will have. There is an aristocracy of soul and there are among the moving mass of people, those who were born for special work, and who have accomplished that work. When in that life, I used to look upon the subject of Mesmerism as one of the things to be let alone. Now I see, under this new light, that no one can afford to let it alone, and that it enters largely or should, into Mental Therapeutics.

If the power used to make people believe that a broom is a fine-toned musical instrument—a piece of twine, a wide and deep river—a minister of the Gospel, a thief, who should be immediately brought to justice—a little child magnified into a queen of some foreign conntry—a black cat into a white elephant, was utilized in the effort to heal the souls and bodies of the people, great results might follow.

But this much abused science, let loose upon a world of people, who are waiting to lean their weary heads on some one, casts the shame of a blameful life on some other object outside their own personality. The thought of its being possible to commit murder and then not be the murderer, is making it necessary for a new course to be taken upon this subject.

Hypnotism as now practised for the amusement of the people does more harm than good. It heals no body—it cures no diseased mind—it is simply the amusement of an hour, but leaving with some the troubles of a life time.

PROF. CADWELL AND HYPNOTISM.

I have made it a pleasant duty to interview Prof. J. W. Cadwell, well known all over the eastern states, upon his present views of Hypnotism, and was not surprised to hear him say, "I used that power as a plaything, which rightly understood, might have borne rich fruits for state and nation."

In my long talk with him, he coincided with my belief that it should be brought before the world in a dignified and respectable manner, and recognized as a great factor in good government—that colleges should be established, where this power of mind over mind, and mind over matter could be studied in all its phases—that diplomas should be given to successful graduates from these schools, making it lawful for them to practice, after a thorough investigation, if their moral lives and bodily habits were in keeping with the high and holy purposes for which an all-wise Power intended the gift. "I see since my transition that there surely was a strong reason for the suppression of mixed gatherings for the display of this gift. For from many of them have gone forth those having a smattering of the power, who try their will over some one for their own aggrandizement. It may be to obtain a loan of money, knowing they never can pay it—the turning of one member of a family against another—the getting some temperance reformer to take the drink that will start him on the downward way and ruin him for public work, or this power may be used to ruin some girl whose life had before been blameless, and numberless other evils that I cannot mention now.

I did treat some patients with my power and helped them, but the world was not ready for the revelation which has since come through study of this great subject."

"How would you guard against the evils resulting from indiscriminate use of this power?"

"I would have all the young people instructed that the influence of any person, who all at once, or by degrees, makes it less easy to do right, and easier to do wrong without compunction of conscience, is a person who is not merely influencing them, but dominating them, and there is danger every step of the way.

There are mental gymnasiums where the thoughts of individuals are felt before they are spoken. I would have all, such apt students that it could not be possible for evil thoughts to make an impression, while good thoughts should make a lasting impression. The power of the mind over the body, so that a patient feels sure that his body will feel nothing during a surgical operation, ought to be sufficient evidence of how much of weal or woe may center in the dominating power of the hypnotist.

There are to-day, thousands of people, poor because minds have dominated them, with the belief that some fortunate mining scheme would bring great wealth to themselves; and hundreds of rascals rich, because they had the power to play upon the minds of their victims. There are scenes in many homes, because the wife has run up great bills which her husband must pay or a fuss will be made, purchases, which would never have been made were it not for the hypnotic influence of the salesman.

There has many a wife signed papers under the spell of hypnotic persuasion, which later on has robbed her of her home.

The ranks of the intemperate are constantly being filled by those who are led by this misdirected power. Laws that are a shame to the nation are often the results of what is called strong, magnetic speeches by some one in the assembly or senate.

The maker of these speeches, either consciously or not, throws out the power, and a nation or state suffers from the influence of one man."

How should Hypnotism be used?

I left Prof. Cadwell with a great query in my mind. How shall the world utilize Hypnotism, and how shall people be guarded against its misuse?

Education seems to be the only lever to be used, and if your world wakes up to the thought of it, it may banish the life-long bug bear of heredity, by creating a right inheritance. It will say to the young mother, "Create your child; nothing can harm it; no sin shall cast its blight over it; live well yourself; think pure thoughts; cast from your mind all undesirable inherited traits on either side; they shall not touch your child." Allow no one to see the mother, who will cast doubt over it, or fear, or voice one note of despondency. Live in the belief that the child shall be free from taint, and even the sins of the fathers will have little or no influence over it.

The above is a theory I should like to see actualized; but upon this side these opinions are much favored. It would do no harm to interest young women who are to be mothers, upon these points. It could not harm the child, for the mother to believe in it, during pregnancy. Of one thing I am sure, that your world and ours, so far as I have seen, are now only on the threshold of spiritual enlightenment, and that the only way to gain the heights desired, is to be on the alert in all ways; spurning nothing that appeals to you for investigation, remembering that the great "Universal Good" has not left out of the economy of nature, one thought or stepping stone for the betterment of humanity.

But it is the work of the spirit of man to divest even that which seems grotesque of its strange habiliments, if concealed beneath, there be one germ of the truth. Great good will only come to the real student. Those who follow their own ideas, although they may bring great gain, cannot receive the blessing of conquest over a hidden truth.

Edison a great Hypnotic Subject.

Edison, the greatest hypnotic subject the modern world has known, has his operators almost entirely in the spirit world; and is reproducing in large degree that which is considered new. Could I give you the real story of what I have learned of of ancient living and thinking, it would rival the the stories of the lost Atlantis, and people this continent with a race as superior in thought, stature and power of invention over you of to-day, as your times are superior to that of the wooden canoe and painted faces of the Indian dwellers upon your soil.

The thought that life is constantly tending upward in some direction, may be true, but that it moves in cycles of development, seems more true, and faithfully corroborates the old saying, "There is no new thing under the sun."

S. Bowles.

PAPER X.
THE SPIRITUALISTIC FIELD.

As I see it now, special attention is at present being paid your world by logical spirits upon this side to find the present status of Spiritualism.

"What can it mean?" say some who are viewing the work there with fearful hearts. "This changing scene—this disbanding of societies—this going into the ranks of the churches, notably the Unitarian—many people who know that spirit communion is a fact."

I answer, one solution of it is,

JESUIT SPIRITS ARE IN IT!

They are calling together but to scatter—lifting up but to let fall again—putting before the public, lights which are electric in their power, for a time, only to let them fade away, obscured by doubt and ignored by their former followers. Phases of mediumship which used to stand perfect test conditions, are now put before the public with fear and trembling, and no person admitted who does not bring an introduction from some well-known friend.

The public is justly growing more critical. True Spiritualists are claiming continued evidence, instead of resting all their belief and knowledge upon the history of past.

A veteran Spiritualist, who had lately entered upon spirit life, said to me, "Although this life is more than I could have hoped for, in the sense that every thing is so beautiful here, yet I have brought with me a deep regret that I was not more discreet in advice to unbelievers. More than twenty years ago, I saw materialization under right test conditions. My people came to me with their own faces, with their own knowledge of events, and talked and walked with me—no gauzy veils to obcure them—no machinery to obscure the light. I could see, hear, feel and knew I had found my own. That satisfied me. I lived upon the thought for years and rehearsed my experiences, but I went only to that one medium for that kind of manifestation.

During the years, I interested friends in my story. When the chance came to visit a medium in a nearby town, I advised my friends to go and see their friends—to have no doubt about it—not to go through with any preliminary stages—just to go and see them.

One after another went and came back only to tell me of their disgust. They saw nothing only what might have been done by one person, without accomplices.

I was offended, and I decided to go myself, taking with me the widow of a prominent man, who had lately passed on. I thought the former visitors were blockheads. Materialization was true.

In the seance room we found lots of fixings, which I had not seen in the old days. It was so dark that I could not see my friend's face, near me. "I wouldn't know my mother in this light," I said.

"Your eyes will soon become accustomed to it," said the medium from the cabinet. "Now sing something loud and clear—be earnest in it."

They sang; the curtains parted and there was something white, visible between them. A form stepped out and some one jerked the light until it almost went out. A faint voice called for one of the circle, who went up. I heard kissing and whispering; and then he came back and said it was his wife. Others went up, until at last my friend was called up, and after a little, screamed out in terror!

They tried to get the forces together again, but they could not, though they sang the "Sweet By and By," very loud.

The medium said it was useless; while my friend, trembling and suffering from a first experience was begging to go home.

"I am afraid to stay," said she; and we left.

"What were you afraid of? I asked. "If it was a spirit, it could not hurt you."

"I am not afraid of spirits, but I am afraid of that man behind those curtains. When I went up, a form of a man not unlike my husband, as nearly as I could see by the dim light, stood there. He whispered to me, calling me by name, and kissing me in an awfully human way. Still I did not know but it was he. His hair was exactly like my husband's—a mass of curls all over his head. I said 'O, Charlie! is this you?' I reached up to caress his curls as I used to, when he was alive. But the man jerked my arm away and somehow I held on to the hair and had a wig in my hands. He then pinched my hands to make me drop it, and then informed the circle that I was hysterical and caused the form to dematerialize suddenly, which had been a shock to the medium."

I did not know whether modern spirits began to dematerialize at the head or the feet. But my friend says she had hold of a wig, and I believe it.

The medium didn't stay much longer in that vicinity. He went away to find others for victims. "What I regret about it,"continued the old man, " is this—I didn't keep up with the times. I didn't read enough; I didn't go enough to find out what goods were being put upon the market—and most of all, I regret that I did not advise people to see phenomena in its simpler phases, reserving materialization for subsequent investigation. "

I felt great sympathy for the man, and told him there would yet be a chance for him to correct the mistake; perhaps by communicating through some simpler phases of mediumship, to his friends who had by following his advice, been disgusted.

"The Lord only knows, " was his response, as he passed out of my presence.

There are thousands of Spiritualists, living in the past of Spiritualism, who should be alive to its onward march to-day ; and equally alive to the humbuggery, which like barnacles, is clinging to it.

Mr. Bowles endorses the National Organization.

I have been pleased to note the progress of a National Organization, through great discouragements. I know that its object is a benevolent one; but the lack of a proper education in this matter, is making it hard for any organization to exist.

Not long ago, at a meeting in one of our large cities, where anti-organization was the theme, one speaker, with great unction, declared that "Blackbirds flew in flocks, while Eagles soared alone." He likened each one upon whom the spiritual light had fallen, to the eagle in strength and power. He further said that the fetters of organization could not bind them.

But at this time, organization of town, county, state and nation is needed. Had it not been for your spiritual organization, with its vigilant leaders and workers, I fear that large classes of people would to-day rejoice because they had succeeded in putting God into the Constitution. Sufficient help is not being given the National Organization; and Spiritualism suffers because of the lack of concentrated action.

The foes to fight are not entirely of your life, for there are spirit enemies constantly at work to produce disruption and fierce antagonism. Societies place upon their platforms those whose lives are as dark as the night. If they are only mediums, if they can give tests, or speak to please the public, such persons are employed. They may do their public work well for the month's engagement. People become interested and then there follows after them, a trail of slime and corruption.

They are not honest in their mediumship, nor pure in their social life. In fact, they should never have been teachers until they had learned the lessons of true mediumship and the necessity of banishing from themselves even the appearance of evil.

Demand clean records, and pure moral conduct of all public speakers and mediums. Those who have seen their mistaken lives and striven by earnest effort in right directions to correct the past, should be encouraged. But if one shred of the old life plague is left, it will spring up and again set in motion those tendencies considered extinct.

It is not necessary to be unkind, but it is necessary to protect that banner of truth which is the enlightening power of the world. The thinkers of the spirit world commend all efforts in any direction that tend toward the harmonizing effect of successful co-operation, and the future of Spiritualism depends upon the course taken by its exponents to-day whether they scatter or bind together, by this scientific religion of the soul.

New phases are coming to light, new mediumship is being developed or at least, new to this century, but that which has had its existence for ages.

The reason for the idea of psychometric reading becoming so prevalent, is that there are spirits overseeing this phenomena, expecting in the near future to develop some medium so that the touch of an article will make it possible for the medium to directly tell the name of the person who owns the article, and from that tell of the spirit friends called by that slight magnetic link between the earthly and the heavenly; and be able to definitely state their present condition and give to the world sure testimony of the presence of the spirit, without any of the trance conditions which are so largely misunderstood by the skeptical investigator.

S. Bowles.

PAPER XI.

IN THE REALM CELESTIAL.

Some seventeen years ago, I believe, I made a statement that it was impossible for me to exist in the higher spheres; and at that time it would have been, even for a moment. I had not learned the secret of spiritual altitudes, and have as yet, only a meager knowledge of it. Still I have for some time been desirous of entering even for a little while, the Realm Celestial.

This was a most important event for me; and I thought, what guide shall I choose to show me the way. At last I asked Mary if she would go.

She said, "No, Samuel, I am not a reporter nor a journalist. They dare go anywhere, but as for me, I think the purity of that realm would make me so ashamed of my unworthy self that I should take no comfort.

My guide asked me, "Whom would you prefer to visit in the Realm Celestial?" (The seventh sphere some call it, but really when you have reached that altitude, the thought of spheres is almost annihilated.)

I said, "I want to visit some common person, one who belonged to the rank and file of life—one who had not been honored publicly. I want to see such a person, for I hope the interview will reach thousands of homes in the earth-world, and be read those who are weary and troubled about many things. Should I visit a great personage, and write up his life in that realm, the people of earth life would say, 'Oh, it was easy for him to climb; he had the world at his feet while on the earth, and it opened the way for him.'

So, just show me one of the home keepers of earth life, translated to that realm, so much talked about and so little understood." He took my arm and we gradually rose up higher and higher on an inclined plane. At first it seemed I must step or make some motion with my feet, but gradually I lost all inclination to do so and was carried along.

The upper air was not an unpeopled country. As on the ladder of old, angels were ascending and descending, so we met hundreds of happy-faced, angelic looking beings, going downward on errands of mercy. At last, my guide stopped and asked me to look around the City Celestial. I gazed as one enraptured. I saw no crowded city with high walls, but a place more like a thickly settled part of the country—and such a view as was opened out to my astonished eyes! Homes everywhere, and such homes as would baffle the descriptive power of the most graphic writer.

I looked at the ground upon which my feet seemed to stand and fancied my heavy weight would break it through, as it appeared to pulsate to the touch of my feet.

"You will feel better floating than walking," said my guide "since you have such a sense of insecurity." So hand in hand we went past these homes, embowered in clinging vines and from which hung the most beautiful flowers. I noticed that each home had different shapes of flowers, and presented different colorings. I asked my guide the cause, as there were appearing to my view, new shades of color, unseen in the lower spheres.

"Those colors on the vines are the expression of the spiritual development of the people who occupy the homes they embower." he said.

"Do you see that mansion yonder, with the dark red color prevailing? The one who dwells there, although beautiful enough to be a resident of the Realm Celestial, and good enough to be here, one whose life had been full of pomp and power in the past—one who was a martyr in earth life, is not yet emancipated from the thought that she was once a queen, and so the color red, which links her most closely with the old life, is around her. I heard her say once, 'Oh! that I could forget those days when I was full of power, bowed down to, praised by a thousand tongues, and only remember that my life was sacrificed for a principle. Over here I could do better work, and then my red roses of power would change to the white blossoms of purity.'"

"O, see those golden bells that hang from the vines over your mansion," I said to one, "What does that mean?"

"It means that I cannot forget I led in the mad race for gold, hundreds of years ago, and if I found it dross, the memory still clings to me."

To the owner of another home I said, "The blue, what does that mean?"

"I wrote poems that lived after me. I am loved yet because God gave me the gift of the poet."

"What does that massive structure mean, covered with flowers of so many shades of green"?

"It means, I was an historian. I have left behind me, massive books for a world to read. I am glad that it was so."

To another, I said, "The changing hues from heliotrope to lavender, what does that mean?"

"The gift of song was mine. I awoke the good in human nature. I inspired genius. I gave wings to hope. I made the miserable, happy, if only for an hour."

To another I said, "That strange blending of colors which I cannot name—that change from the darkest shades to shimmering, silvery whiteness at the edges of the leaves —What does that mean?"

"I was one of the old masters, and with me died the secret of wonderful coloring—of shades that live, though those of nature die; of the power to create color by skillful manipulations; it was mine."

"And here we see where absence of all color makes a strong contrast to the rest; what of the occupants of that modest dwelling? See how the white bells hang down almost transparent and the green leaves seem as though a breath would blow them away."

"But a breath will not blow them away. They change from old to new, but are not destroyed nor made unsightly. Those flowers mean, "Through much tribulation, I gained the City Celestial."

"This is one of the most beautiful in this section," said my guide, pointing in another direction.

and as I gazed upon it and saw the wondrous beauty of the home, and the curving of leaf and flower, I felt like falling in adoration before a power that could create such garlands of beauty. The blossoms were five leaved, rather small and white as wax. The center of each flower had little stamens, upon which glittered diamond like anthers. I looked again and again.

"It dazzles me," I said, "I cannot look long, but oh! what beauty."

"It is because your eyes are not accustomed to the City Celestial," he said.

"The occupant of this home is the one I desire you to see, one of the common people of the earth. I will ascertain if she will receive you."

"Angelia, will you receive this friend, once of the mortal world and tell him of your life?"

If I could only describe her who stood before me, with such noble bearing, yet with such an angelic face! If I could tell you of hair like fine-spun gold, in waves of light, that seemed constantly changing its hue! If I could tell you of that form, magnificent in proportions, yet having apparently no weight, and the garments that were a revelation in themselves! Every change of position gave a different impression of the glittering white surface, and yet every motion was as unstudied as that of a child.

"Be seated," said she with a voice like silver bells.

I looked around to the place where my guide had stood, but he was gone, and then I looked helplessly to the proffered seat. I could see right through it, and I thought it would not bear my weight. I who had felt so light a little while before, now felt as though I was experiencing all the difficulties of earthly avoirdupoise.

She smiled and said, " Sit down, the seat will hold you; you are not as heavy as you think;" and so I dared to risk it. The seat, seemed in some subtle way to adapt itself to my proportions; and I was at once at ease in the presence of this regal angel of light.

"Of what would you have me speak," said she, though I think she must have known without asking me, for she looked me through and through.

I answered "I wish to learn of your earth life and how you gained your present position."

"I was a peasant's wife in far off Italy. I knew of only trouble and care. There were children, so many of them I did not know what to do; and then my sister died and I added her three to my five, and the home was so full. My husband worked hard, and he blamed me because I added more burdens to him; but the good God gave me strength, and I taught the little ones to till the land and help me.

Then my husband came over to this life and I suffered much from fear I had been selfish after all, and added to his burdens, instead of being kind in taking my sister's orphans.

That weighed upon my mind so much that I was very unhappy until one night a dream came to me. I was told in the vision, (for now I know it was one) not to let my heart be troubled, but to live as best I could, and teach all the children the sin of untruth, make their lives just as spotless as I could, and that it would be well with me.

Some of them were very hard to teach. I could not find in my poor Catholic faith, that which I wished to teach them, and so when I worked in the vineyards, dug in the earth, planted the vines, or sowed the grain, there came to me, sweet thoughts that I made (now I see it) shine out of my life into theirs, and my oldest boy often caught my thought and was the inspiration to a king whom he afterwards served. The king let this kind light shine over his kingdom and each one of those children entered some avenue in life which helped to spread the light which had come to me, until it was over seas and in many climes.

That was my first stepping stone to the Celestial Realm. I lived in earth life to be very old as they call it. I laugh now at the thought of age. I was wrinkled and bent and I suffered. My children were far away, but came sometimes, begging me to go home with them; but I would not go. 'I wanted to stay in the little home until I died,' I said, and they went away sorrowfully to their duties.

Away back in my rosy youth, I had an enemy. She had envied me and robbed me of my lover, for all life seemed sweeter for his having lived. She did not get him herself, but she had cast a shadow over my young life, so I never felt quite as I did before, and still I tried to do my duty. She came to me in her last days, more wretched, more suffering than I could have thought of being I took her in, and when I came to this life, I begged my children to let her stay in my old cottage till she too entered the higher life, to use my savings, and she did. 'If thine enemy is homeless give him shelter,' some wise one had said, and I remembered it.

That was my second step to the City Celestial. Well, after I was in the first sphere of spirit life, I began to see that I had not done my duty —no, not all of it. I was at first restful in the work of the past. When I was awakened to just what I was and all that surrounded me, and what I must do, I prayed for knowledge—I was so untutored—I wanted to speak in different tongues. That was granted me, and thereby I could do more efficient work—and Oh! the work I wanted to do, which I could not do. I was so eager to cleanse my own heart that I might help the earth world to sin less.

I did not know there was so much of wrong in in the whole world, but I looked back and was comforted, for my grandchildren were working more and more in the line of my childhood's work, and I was told to keep comforting those who came over, hoping to find the Celestial City at once.

'I do not know what the Celestial City is,' I said, to one who called to Jesus to help her, to carry her past, all that was gross, to the good God on his throne; and then I found that those who came from your life, could not understand that the description of the kingdom was only an imperfect vision of an imperfect man; and that even in the soul realm one must work for it.

I found people, waiting for the master to guide them over into the new Jerusalem, and I found they had been violators of the law, and thought they had been forgiven; and Oh! such sad lessons as they had to learn. Then I found those who had not been violators of the law. They were not criminals nor outcasts, but had faithfully adhered to their religious creeds. But still they had only lived by the letter of the law; they knew not the spirit, so I was one to help them to see the difference.

Then I found those who must yet have lessons in the shadows. They had not reached a place where they could stand the light.

And thus from sphere to sphere, through wonderful gradations, was I led to this my present home. My task was to teach the mission of sorrow to spirits until they could hear the songs of immortal life. But it has been a happy life all the way, since my transition. Some have said, 'Stop and rest, why toil so much?'

And I would answer, 'I seek a city ye have not seen.' When I found what my life had builded for me, I said, 'I will inspire from my sweet home, all hearts with the thought of unselfishness.'

Now I am studying the Infinite—I am watching the worlds move round—I am trying to understand what law means and how it acts—I am watching among the glorified, the upward steps yet to be taken, and watching to see what new revelations will be brought to view. I did not rest until I entered the Realm Celestial, and at times I feel I must rest no longer. But those who have been here many years, tell me to bide yet awhile, for I will have yet many chances, such as I have to-day, to send word down to the lower spheres and to mortals—that it is not wealth—it is not power—it is not knowledge only, which gives us the key to the 'Gate of the Celestial

City'; but it is honest work—honest aspiration and a willingness to leave all things for the glory of the truth."

I asked her no questions. What could I ask that regal woman? Then a sudden feeling of uncertainty warned me that I was losing power over myself, and I sought my guide. He awaited me, and I went gladly to my quiet home in the fifth sphere.

"One cannot be a dweller in the Realm Celestial, Mary," I said as I threw myself upon a couch, which I knew would not break beneath my weight, until he has become much more spiritual than I am."

"That's what I thought," said she, smiling. But afterwards, when I described it to her, she said, "We'll watch the children, won't we? and all the loved ones. The Realm Celestial will be enduring, and we shall reach it by and by."

S. Bowles.

PAPER XII.

AN INTERVIEW WITH LUCY STONE ON HER PRESENT IDEAS OF WOMAN SUFFRAGE.

I think no one will deny that in earth life, I was interested in all questions of a reformatory nature. The Woman Suffrage question in its incipient stages, at first thrilled me with disgust, and then with an interest which deepened as the years went by. I, at first, thought with the disdain of strong manhood, of homes that it would change—how the young, loving mother would almost assume the appearance of coarseness, were she to become a voter.

Voting and being feminine were paradoxical to my mind. Our homes would be peopled by a set of office seekers, who would nearly make orphans of our children, and spoil the sacredness of home life.

But when Susan B. Anthony showed so truly one side of the picture, and Lucy Stone showed the strong yet gentle side of it, I began to think there was no reason why the same rights of men should not be extended to women.

This belief, although I did not give it the publicity which I now wish I had, strengthened with the need, as viewed from a political stand-point.

What George Wm. Curtis, that noble man of letters and believer in equal rights, said, years ago, is still true,—"The opposition to woman suffrage is only a repetition of traditional prejudice, the product of mere sentimentality; and to cope with it, is like wrestling with a malaria, or arguing with the east wind." Yet from this side, he and I and hundreds of others, deeply interested, are watching states as they come under this banner of woman's enfranchisement and are wondering how long the state upon whose shores the seekers for freedom first landed, a state foremost in reforms, open-handed to sufferers in any calamity—a state whose statesmen cry out loud against monopolies which rob the people, will allow this greatest monopoly of all, that of the ballot box, to go on. God grant it will not be long before the women of every state will arouse to the thought that there are public duties to perform, as well as duties to the home and to the church. The most humiliating of all thoughts connected with the subject, is, that woman should have to ask of man that which should be her right.

I was in those early days deeply interested in the burning words and brilliant genius of Alexander Hamilton, who in the New York Legislature, said to a committee that had found no proper precedent for woman's enfranchisment, as nearly as I can recall it, 'The sacred rights of humanity are not to be rummaged for, among old parchments or dusty records. They are written as with a sunbeam, on the whole volume of human nature, by the hand of Divinity itself, and cannot be obscured or erased by mortal power!'

The rights most talked of in Jeffersonian days were natural rights, without regard to sex. A woman has the same right to life and liberty that a man has, and should have the same rights about property; but as yet, in many states, ignorant, taxless men may vote for expenditures, unnecessary and extravagant, where the protest of one who must make the real sacrifice is of no avail.

Every one is disgusted, whether aware of it or not when other people, without consulting them, take upon themselves unlimited power to regulate their course in life.

LUCY STONE STILL AT WORK.

Alive with this thought, I sought the home of Lucy Stone. I found her busy as ever in work that will tell. She greeted me as an old acquaintance and in her matter of fact way, said,—

"I am glad to see you—glad to know that now at least, you must thoroughly coincide with this thought of mine—the thought of earth—the inspiration of heaven."

I assured her of my sympathy, and she said,— "Mr. Bowles, sympathy is a good thing; but in the earth life it was a wicked waste. The number of people on the earth plane who have said they sympathized with us and would like to help us, only some of their friends held them back, is legion. They proved to be the heavy weights which the suffrage cause had to carry on its back for fear of losing one element of usefulness.

Could I speak to them now as I want to, I would say, 'Go ahead! The person who sympathizes and does nothing, is not one of your kind and will never help the cause until it becomes popular, and then we shall not need them.'"

'Haven't you reached your people,?" I asked, noticing the wistfulness that came into her face.

"No, not as satisfactorily as I could wish. They asked me if I would come back or send word, just before the last of earth life, and I think I said, 'I shall be too busy.' But now I see this spiritual field is the one to work in if one can only have the chance. Though I knew of this philosophy, I am crippled in communicating and do not as I desire, reach my best beloved. I want them to see me as I am; more like the Oberlin student than the worn and weary woman who spent her life in the development of a cause, yet hated and rebelled against, even by those to whom it gives justice and helpfulness."

"What is your opinion of the present development of the suffrage cause?"

"Its growing now," said she, brightening up, because women as well as men are becoming students in this great problem. Men don't think they are selfish, they don't mean to be—but they are not generous enough or wise enough to legislate fairly for women, because legislation is usually in favor of the legislating class, and that shuts women out almost entirely from the rights which her nature would most surely prize as hers—hers to be cared for—her right to keep herself unsullied. It is not safe to one class of citizens to trust another class with all political power."

"Would it not in most families, be true that the wife's vote would be an echo of her husband's?"

"No; I do not believe it would, unless that husband was on the side that the wife, after careful study, deemed the just side. Some of them doubtless would have husbands like Gov. Orr of South Carolina, who said, 'The rights of freedmen would be safest in the hands of their old masters.' There might be many who would strive to monopolize the rights of women, even after the edict for emancipation had gone forth.

But this great wave of educational force which has touched the brain of the farm woman in the rural districts as well as in the fashionable home, will enlighten the women as rapidly as it does the men.

If every woman would answer every man who asks this question, 'What do you want the ballot for?' with a like one, 'What do men want the ballot for?' and both give reasons, the reasons would be kindred ones."

"What States do you think will be first to give the ballot to woman?"

"More of the Western States.—

'Westward the star of Empire takes its way,' the poet sang, and now it seems to be travelling back in a new form."

"What hinders Massachusetts from falling in line with this reform?"

"The fear of a new dispensation, with politicians, a cleaning-house time, when all old rubbish will have an airing—and another class who argue 'the time is not ripe—create a public sentiment—be patient—educate yourselves.'

Another class, (mainly women and ministers,) imagine that somewhere in Holy Writ, there is a prohibitory law against allowing a woman to act in any other capacity than as a wife or servant of man.

People don't believe enough in the good judgment of women. They imagine it is protection to keep political care from women, when burdens that would stagger men, are constantly her lot to bear.

But America is a disturber of traditions; and the record of the century which is now closing, and of the new one coming, will be that of the combined efforts of men and women for laws which will educate and protect."

"What wonders will women work out in legislation when the ballot is in their hands?"

"I do not suppose that the zealous women consider that they would be so much wiser than their brothers, but there is one thing which I think would come to pass. To be a woman is in many ways, to have a keener sense of human needs. To be a mother, is to adopt into your soul the world of boys and girls. A man loves his children and theorizes: but she who bore them, acts.

There are gambling houses, brothels and grogshops on every corner. Somebody's boy is going into them."

Her hands clasped, convulsively; "Oh! if it was my boy! Is there no law to prevent a girl, under the influence of the first liquor ever tasted, being led away to her ruin? 'What if it is my girl?' says the shuddering woman; and she thinks of the time when with our added shower of ballots, crime will be made less easy, and a more perfect education will banish in part, hereditary tendencies that make desolate, human hearts.

But if all the liquor should continue to be used that is now used—if maidens continue to be sacrificed upon the altar of lust—if corruption in courts should remain the same—if all the evils which now exist, should still exist, still I would say in the name of human justice, give to woman the ballot: let her do her part—bear her responsibility with those who make better or worse, the history of our loved Republic."

I fear I have not quoted her in all respects correctly. If word for word was reported as uttered, you would have no conception of their force, for you did not see this marvellous woman of two worlds as she uttered them—such eagerness—such flashes of light from a face illumined with a great truth—such hope—such courage for womankind expressed in word and action by Lucy Stone, the heavenly leader of an earthly reform.

SAMUEL BOWLES.

PAPER XIII.

Two ways of understanding Prayer.

The subject of my morning thought to you explains in a measure, itself, and yet I would further explain. It is the way you of earth life understand it and how we of this higher realm understand it, in the light of a higher education.

There had been considerable discussion upon the subject by a number of friends that almost daily convened for interchange of thought. We concluded that we would each visit a church or religious society on your earthly Sabbath—each one to go to a different city and hear the prayers; at the same time looking into the minds of those who offered the prayers, to see what ambition prompted them.

There were seven of us. I will relate my experience first, and designate the others by the first six letters of the alphabet.

A Horse Jockey—Auctioneer Revivalist.

My attention has of late been drawn to one who is considered a great exponent of the truth, one who is instrumental in saving souls, one who is known in every state in the Union. At this time he was in Cincinnati, Ohio.

I found myself in one of the largest churches in the city, and it was crowded to the doors. The minister of the church had a seat in the pulpit and gave out the hymns, for they were to have congregational singing.

A man of exceedingly strange appearance arose. He seemed to be a cross between a horse-jockey and an auctioneer. His first remark on rising to his feet, was this.—

"When I'm hired to do a job, I want to make a clean business of it—don't care to have people do my prayin'. I know what God ought to do for us to-day, so I am goin ter pray that the work will be done ter day, not next week, nor next month. Let us pray.

'O! God, we come ter you ter-day ter get somethin and we are goin ter have it. We want in purtikler the soul of a rich man in this congregation, which we know ought to be saved. We don't want any foolin about it. Put the clinchers rite on him, and make him know that we know the Devil calls him his own! O! Lord, give him the feelin that you know where he was last night and his awful deal with Satan! Show him that he's railroading strait toward hell! Show him if he had a million more of rail-road stocks, he could'nt buy a moment of time! Show him the faces of some of his friends who have gone ter hell, lately. Make this your purtiklar work to-day, and do the best yer can for the rest of these sinners in silks and satins who ought to be in sackcloth and ashes!'"

He prayed in the same strain for some time. I drew closer and closer to him—worked my way past clownish-looking spirits, who with coarse jests, tried to impede my progress.

I was determined, and read the mind of that man while the audience was singing. "Hit 'im too hard I guess. The old cuss don't look as though he thought I meant him. I ought to have explained a little more about what he was doin': then may be, he would come down with the cash, so they'd keep me another week. Well, well, I must get at it," he said to himself, as the audience ceased singing.

Who of the unseen ones had heard his prayer?

Those of his own kind, who were in sympathy with him in his unholy work, would perhaps work in a way to answer his prayer for the sake of money.

I left him, sad and disgusted that aught which had ever been considered holy, should have fallen so low.

THE PRESBYTERIAN SERVICE.

Mr. A—— was next called upon. He said, "I was brought up in the Presbyterian faith, and the prayers and services of that church were all of truth to me. I would not believe I could have so changed and they have moved forward so little.

It was a small church in a suburb of the now large city of Pittsburg, Pa. It was a village which seemed far away from the city when I was young; but it has crept that way. No familiar faces were to be seen in the old church, now modernized.

A middle-aged, dyspeptic looking clergyman occupied the pulpit. There were hard lines upon his face, placed there by keeping all the points of the law in his mind and forgetting all points of love.

He began by praying thus:—"Oh! thou Infinite and Everlasting God, Thou to whom all nations bow, hear us, we beseech Thee, this morning, while we ask Thee to hasten the time when Thy elected shall know Thy face. Make them to feel the time spent in iniquity is their great loss—that they had best be about their Father's work. Put away from their minds, greed for earthly treasure, and if they have been blessed with riches, may they lay it all at Thy feet. Bless the church of the living God. Add to its membership. Be with the sick. Bless the poor and forsaken, and finally gather Thy children into Thy kingdom, for Christ, the Redeemer's sake, Amen.'

I, like brother Bowles, pushed my way forward, touched his brain and read his thought. "Well, I know one thing; there must be more paying members in this church or I shall have to take my family and go somewhere else."

He seemed to be an honest man, and he really thought he believed in the doctrine of foreordination, and desired that more from that number might come into the church, for the support of the church. They would be saved at last. It was only a question of time, but haste was better than delay."

THE SPIRITUALIST MEETING.

Mr. B—— then gave his experience. "I was drawn to the great city of Chicago and being interested in the promulgation of that which is termed in the earth world, Spiritualism, I found myself in a large building, more like a theater than like a church, where a crowd was gathered to listen to the inspiration of their speaker. She began as nearly as I can remember, by saying:—

'Oh! Thou, the Author of all Being, Infinite and Eternal God. Life of all souls; Life of all Intelligence; Source of all truth; Thou ever living Fountain of love; unto Thee the nations turn and Thy children worship Thee at the shrine of prayer to-day. May all aggressiveness be turned to fraternity. May human hearts learn the manifestation of that fraternity through Thee.'

I could not remember the whole prayer. It was not indefinite if one believed in a personal God, but except one did, it would be hard to fathom the meaning of this prayer.

I found her brain so encircled by people from this side, of many different orders of faith, yet all having the God idea, that I could not clearly sense the real thought of the Instrument. I listened also to her address which was of a high order of inspiration, but for that day did not seem as practical as I could have desired for human needs."

THE CHURCH OF THE DIVINE PATERNITY.

Mr. C—— said, "I have been more fortunate than any of you. I found in the city of New York, something that harmonized with my idea of prayer. The Church of the Divine Paternity, I believe was the name of the organization. The Pastor was a middle-aged man. After an anthem had been sung, he said:—

'Oh! Thou Invisible Force, whom men call God: Thou, who workest in Thine own way, touching the souls of men. Help us to-day to do good—to be helpful, to be guides to strengthen souls. Send the the message of thy love down to the lonely and forsaken ones. Move each heart here to know that no true prayer can be answered which will not alleviate human suffering. Move each one during some portion of the time, to-day, to give thanks for earthly bounties, by practically feeding the hungry, and clothing the cold; by giving comfort to the sick and afflicted. May this Sabbath be rounded out in its fullness of blessing, by spending some time in blessing others; and thus may they imitate Him who went about doing good. Amen."

"I looked into that man's mind and found he meant what he prayed. I looked into the faces of the people, made beautiful because of a tender sympathy, and saw the resolves to do some good before evening should come. I did not stay to watch results, but I believe that man's prayer was answered."

The Old-Fashioned Methodist Meeting.

Mr. D—— said, "I visited an old-fashioned Methodist meeting in an unfashionable part of the city of Buffalo, N. Y. The minister was short, fat and full of glory. He knelt down upon the floor instead of a cushion, and thus addressed the Lord :—

"Oh! Lord, we have been trying to save the people and build up thy kingdom. Wilt Thou not this morning, unstop the deaf ears and unseal the blind eyes of those who are going straight to destruction? Save them, save them, Oh! Lord. Thou canst do all things. Thou canst turn all hearts to Thee. Reach these poor worms of the dust, and Oh! Lord, may they know that it rests with them, that all the blood of the Lamb, slain on Calvary, cannot save them unless they are willing to be saved. Touch their hearts just now and bring them to Thee."

After the direct contradiction given above, I could listen no longer—telling God He could save them if He wanted to, and then declaring that God Himself could not save them, if they were not willing to be saved. I did not stop to read that man's thoughts; I did not think they would be worth reading, and with the sound of amen, amen, ringing loud upon the air, I left for more congenial quarters."

THE JEWISH SYNAGOGUE.

Mr. E—— said, "I went to a synagogue in Philadelphia and heard a Rabbi pray. He prayed:— 'Oh! God of Israel, gather Thy children together and let them see that the dawn is near. Show them the Messiah cometh to the hearts of men, for our people mourn because so many of our people are wandering down by the cold streams of Babylon.'

I did not listen longer, for I could not understand what he meant. Excuse my meagre report."

THE SALVATION ARMY.

"I went to the meeting of the Salvation army in Syracuse, N. Y." said Mr. F—— "and saw a real answer to prayer. They were shouting as usual, and a half dozen talking at once. My attention was drawn to one poorly-dressed woman in Salvation army dress, whose face could be clearly seen, as she knelt in prayer. She was imploring that her precious boy might be saved from the power of drink. 'Save him, Oh! Lord,' she said, 'he is my all, and melt his heart so he will come to this meeting. Do not let him blame his poor old mother for serving Thee. Bring him to Christ. Bring him to his mother. Spoil the power of Satan to accomplish his ruin.'

I watched her through the prayer. There was so much of agony in her face. I watched a party she could not see—a trio of spirits who compassed her about. They too seemed to be pleading for help from some higher source.

Scarcely had her voice ceased, when a young girl—an angel of light, dressed in pure white, with shining eyes and glad face, led in a young man, who, by his dress and bloated face, showed how low he had fallen. She led him to his mother, who had just risen and was standing.

'I've been outside with the toughs, mother and heard you pray for me, your boy, and I could not help coming to you and saying, I will stop drinking, I will serve God.' I did not stop to hear more, for there was such a noise of prayer and praise. But then I saw an answered prayer—answered by spirit friends, who at that time, had power to respond. My thought was, oh, I hope it will last."

All that we had heard was very interesting. I pondered more deeply than ever upon the subject of prayer. There has been too much of that kind of praying which expects to lie down with good resolutions and be covered with the glory of heroic action. They pray, but do not work.

CHILDREN ARE OFTEN TAUGHT FALSE NOTIONS OF PRAYER.

A minister's little boy, (if I mistake not, this medium knows of the fact) was greatly moved by the idea that he must have a sister. He came into the house one day, and said, "Mamma, does God hear and answer our prayers?"

"Yes, my boy," said the fond mother.

"Then, mamma, come straight into the parlor and pray just what I tell you to pray. Say, 'Dear God, send Roy a little sister, quick.'"

The confused mother, scarce knowing what to to do, repeated the prayer and the boy went to his play, satisfied it would be so, because mamma said God could do all things.

In less than a week, there was a little girl born to that household, and the triumphant child urged every boy who wanted a sister to get his mamma to pray with him and he would get a sweet little sister in a few days.

I think that even scoffers will find that true prayer is that which sets in action the love-force of spirits upon this side, which acts in accordance with law for the betterment of the supplicant.

S. BOWLES.

PAPER XIV.

A VISIT TO ABRAHAM LINCOLN.

"Why is it, Samuel, that you do not take me to visit some of the great people whom you used to visit before I came to you? I hope my coming will not interrupt the researches you were accustomed to make. I would like to go with you to-day. Would a woman be in the way?"

"No; my dear," I replied; "my wife will never be in the way in anything I can do here. I have learned to understand the larger sphere of womankind. Where do you want to go?"

" I want to go and see Mr. Lincoln."

"You have truly chosen a good man," I answered, and at once sent the dispatch over the spiritual line, which informed him of our desire for a special interview. The response was, "Come."

"I am so glad you have let us into the home corner instead of into that immense room you use for your 'wise talks,'" said Mary, as she responded to the kindly welcome given by both Mr. and Mrs. Lincoln.

"I don't make company of any one on this side," said Mrs. Lincoln, cordially, "we are one family here and must feel an individual interest in the happiness of all with whom we come in contact."

Mr. Lincoln conversed very pleasantly for awhile of the new developments for beautifying homes in the spirit world, and for the betterment of those who come into spirit life without a right understanding of what it means—of the great benefit to scientific research, Prof. Tyndall had been in earth life. "I never" said Mr. Lincoln, "shall forget my first visit to him. I was eager to tell him of my admiration for him and for all the scientists of all generations.

He was glad to see me, and spoke of the work I had done, and I thought, magnified my personal influence. While uttering one of his most interesting sentences, he laid back in his chair and went to sleep! Whether to sit still or to go away, I did not know; but in a few moments he quickly awoke.

'Excuse me,' he said, 'did you not know that an incurable insomnia was one of the causes of my transition? It seems so good to rest. I think it will take years to catch up. I sleep in season and out of season; my spiritual brain as well as my earthly brain was robbed of its power.'

'It was your penalty, Professor, for your devotion to the forces of nature. What you have done will live on and on, after the crawling multitude which antagonized you, has passed from earth and their puny spirits are trying to find a ray of light outside the barriers of an early education, which crippled, and a faith which cannot sustain the soul in the crisis of death.'

'Well, I am not content with with my past. I found, with all my best efforts, I was a coward in a measure. I only asserted the half. The realm of ether was open to me, and I did not recognize it sufficiently to build a firm foundation for a magnificent structure.'

'He then fell into a dreamy silence, half awake. His friend and secretary followed me to the door and said, ' You must excuse the Professor ; he can not yet keep awake—he will, after awhile, but sleep opens new worlds to him, and he is not idle.' "

"What of your own life and work, Mr. Lincoln?"

" My own life?" said he, "I feel almost empty-handed. I accomplish so little—such a strange conflict—I cannot understand. My first idea when I came over, was, that I could inspire the workers at Washington—now I regret to admit that our greatest strength has to be spent in controlling their efforts. How have the mighty fallen!

Many years ago, when I was a young man, I visited a slave market in St. Louis, and saw the selling of numbers of slaves on the auction block. I saw young girls handled like animals. Then and there, I brought my fist down and said, 'If I ever get a chance to strike a blow at slavery, I'll strike it hard.' This saying has entered into history. I did not know that it was a dim foreboding of the blow I would strike, but I was only the instrument.

Now some one is needed to strike another blow there; a crushing blow at the system that enslaves so many people. The man with the pick on the railroad is helping to pay for a useless bauble on the breast of a woman. The girl behind the counter, if she is able to live by the sacrifice of her health, without being robbed of her honor, is helping to set the wheels in motion which will weave for some other girl with little of the good sense of the weary clerk, a wondrous fabric, which will adorn without beautifying.

Oh! my friend Bowles, we are devising ways to to reach Capital and Labor, and the money question, and all questions which shall equalize the gifts of life. We have some theories which would revolutionize, but where are the sensitive brains which we can mould? Where are the men in power that we can sway, even though we beseech and pray, and leave our heaven in the hope of gaining even a point for helpless humanity."

"You are discouraged, Mr. Lincoln, are you not, with the present phase of politics? But you know a new reign will soon begin. Are you not hopeful for the result?"

"The same manipulating forces which have been at work, will still be at work there. The tendency is all in one direction—more power for the powerful, greater weakness for the weak—more money for the millionaires—less money for working people, less homes for the poor, more landlords and struggling tenants. Talk of emancipation, Mr. Bowles, the bud was only nipped by the enfranchisement of the African race."

"Are you fearful of another war?"

"Yes, in a way I am. Arbitration with other nations seems far-fetched when the chances for war seem so remote. Let Congress regulate the seething mass in our own nation—giving it the surety of peace instead of a sword—of homes instead of hovels —of brotherly love instead of usurpation of human rights."

"Mr. Lincoln, you are not in this despairing mood all of the time, are you?" asked Mary. "I should think it would spoil your heaven."

"I hav'nt got there yet," said Mr. Lincoln. "I am only waiting for more work to be done. I could not be content with heaven if I left one stone unturned to put out the real fires of hell. I am glad you came. I would like to have you see Garfield and the rest of us, when we are together. They may see better ways for effecting a change than I do and feel more hopeful."

NETTIE COLBURN MAYNARD.

"Oh! how do you do," said Mr. Lincoln, a bright smile irradiating his face. "Let me introduce you to these people. This is Mrs. Nettie Colburn Maynard, through whom the angels helped me to be strong in earth life."

Her face was like the morning! "O! friends," she said, "it is beautiful, just to exist and to be well, to have a body that I can use, to feel no pain—it is more than heaven."

"She is one of our mediums still, Mr. Bowles," explained he. " The higher spirits who send word to us, instead of coming themselves, are quite at home with her, and her marvellous experiences render her very proficient in reading the intentions of people on the earth plane."

"Through great tribulation you have been made victor, " said Mary, softly : "I have heard much of you, and since coming here, have hoped to meet you."

"I am a frequent visitor at this home," said Mrs. Maynard. "I have been made one of the family. I can look ahead and see encouragement where Mr. Lincoln cannot penetrate. So you see I am hopeful and happy : and Pinkie, my Indian girl is seeking when I am quiet, to do something for Spiritualism. Her powers for manifesting are much more marvellous than mine. She has made a study of it more than I have. "

"I am so glad we went," said Mary, "only I did not visit with Mrs. Lincoln half as much as I wanted to. She seemed so preoccupied. I'll try it over again."

We went home and talked it over. Mary said, "If you really think, and Mr. Lincoln thinks there is wrong and treachery and great danger, why don't you through that medium, write such thrilling words, that the people of the United States will be compelled to scatter them broadcast over the nation?"

"Neither will they be persuaded though one rose from the dead," I repeated, slowly. "Mary, did you believe I could pen the loving words I did in my eagerness to reach you of earth life ? "

"No, I did not at first, but the idea grew on me, for I studied, but said little."

"The people down there, are studying and saying nothing. That is what hinders our progress in awakening them to reform society. They say nothing and do nothing. One or two, or perhaps half a dozen printing offices, from which shine forth spiritual lights, because their presses are rolling out spiritual truth for the world, are but tiny bits of leaven in comparison to the mass to be leavened. They do but feeble work, when the work should be so mighty!"

"Well, we will work, won't we?" said Mary.

"Yes, we will."

SAMUEL BOWLES.

PAPER XV.

A Visit to Leland Stanford.

"Where are you going?" asked Mary as she saw me get my note book.

"Nowhere that you will be interested in going," was my answer, "for it may be a dry subject to you, this interviewing a man about his present ideas as compared with past ones in governmental affairs."

"Oh! shame on you! Haven't you already committed yourself upon the subject of woman suffrage? Then why should I not be as much interested in that which pertains to the good of our great nation, as you are? Have not you and I equal interests there? There is that on earth which appeals to me as well as you."

"Well, come at once," said I, " you always get the best of me in a discussion."

Bright and Misty Days in the Spirit World.

The day was delightful. You may wonder that I say this and ask, are not all days delightful there? I answer to you, no. I have never been in so high a sphere yet, but nature's laws were inexorable. Therefore we have days that are misty, not bright; we have at times a chill in the atmosphere that reminds us of the past. We are so sensitive to these conditions that a very small change is felt at once. For a long period I did not sense it perceptibly, as I had in your life been accustomed to them, but now I am sensitive to all changes.

You speak there, very often, of atmospheric conditions affecting the medium so you cannot get what is true; and then again when everything on your side seems right, you fail utterly in results. Why? Because the controlling spirits from this side have not learned that the differences in our spiritual atmosphere, for hours perhaps, has precluded the possibility for intelligent communications. They have not the spiritual electricity to take with them, and it proves almost a case of 'wires being down.' It is a constant study on this side to find out the hindrances to spirit communion.

But I have digressed. As nearly as I can judge, his spirit home is above the University in California, which he established. We found it a delightful place.

Mr. Stanford was not a stranger to me, as I had

seen him in earth life. I was sure of the greeting which awaited us. His home was a bower of roses.

"I like it so, and so does my boy and the rest of the friends. It is the sweetest comfort I take as I lie upon the couch, to hear joyful or hopeful words come to me from my wife—poor woman," said he. "Sometimes I think the burden is more than she can bear, but she is so self-sacrificing, so strong to overcome difficulties, that the desire of my heart as well as hers is, that the education of the children of earth life shall not be interrupted."

He addressed my wife in the most kindly way, and then said, "Friend Bowles, you are almost to be envied to have on this side the inspiration of your life. I wish I could make them realize the cowardice of letting claims rest until a man's body is under the sod—and then settling like a vulture upon that which is left, thinking that woman in her weakness will succumb without standing to the uttermost for her rights; but she I love and trust is brave. She has prayed many a night for me to come and help her, and in the darkness, with earthly shadows added to this mental one, I have lighted the way for her to pursue. There has been injustice done. More will be attempted. Old proofs do not seem forthcoming, (and there is a good reason why). The power of numbers, of a corporation against one woman is pretty rough. I would be satisfied if both sides were thoroughly known, and it would change the scale somewhat of debt and credit.

Pardon me though for striving to entertain you with personal and family affairs, Mr. Bowles, I did not think you might not be interested in them."

"Every body is interested in that which will so greatly effect a University whose name has become a household word," I replied.

STANFORD ON THE MONEY SYSTEM.

"I know what you wish me to talk about before you ask me, he said, smiling. "It is to know my present opinion of the money system of the United States, as compared with my former opinions."

"Yes, that is what I would like to ascertain."

"Well, brother Bowles, I have studied the issues in my mind, and sometimes have doubted the advisability of any of the financial ideas I advocated during my earth life; but with the turn affairs have taken, now, I am almost of the opinion that the policy I advocated in 1890 (I believe) would have been a policy for the people; and made every citizen more entirely the child of the government. I begin to think that my idea of the two per cent interest on values, borrowed from the government, would have given confidence to the agriculturists, and all classes of labor. I think now as then, that legal tender notes could be issued upon both gold and silver, feeling that it is the internal commerce which should receive our first consideration, and that the system of land security would be equal to inexhaustible mines of gold and silver.

I am not a gold man nor a silver man. I do not believe either alone will redeem the country from its deplorable condition. Gold puts the pressure on one side, silver upon the other. The national bank system as I look at it more and more, seems to benefit the stockholders of the concern and that is about all. You pay largely for what you get; you get little for what you deposit.

Man's necessities are his enemies. He must pay to the uttermost when need comes, but what does he get? The more I think of it as I now see it, Mr. Bowles, I would have the National banks abolished, and have the dealings of a nation's people with its own government, carried on by loan bureaus, established by the government.

All are called cranks who utter such heresies, bnt I believe the time will come when this policy will be better understood. I am humiliated when I see the greed manifested there. It appalls me! I know if it is not changed—if this concentration of the money power is not made impossible, our loved country will follow in the path of other countries, which have bowed to the power of this monopoly.

If I remember rightly, Egypt died when ninety seven per cent of her wealth became centered in not more than three per cent of her people. Babylon, still worse, for she fell when ninety eight per cent of her wealth belonged to two per cent of the people. Persia died when one per cent of her people owned the realm; and Rome fell when two thousand of her nobles owned the known earth. I may have mixed the figures. I have not time to hunt it up," said he, looking at the ponderous volumes on the shelves of his library, "but the thought holds good, for to-day that is the tendency. A man who tells the truth is an alarmist, and sometimes he is called more cruel names than that.

The worn grooves of old parties could no longer hold me. If I was now on the earthly side, something newer than the newest thought would have to be evolved, to make me again willing to enter the political arena."

"You were a man of large experience, Mr. Stanford, both as Governor of California and as United States Senator."

"You were known all over the world, and may I ask if you are not at present, deploring some of the methods by which you accumulated your immense wealth?"

Stanford favors Co-operation.

"I knew you would hit me about that, and I am glad of it. Yes, I was in the race, and I think of it now with regret, although I made my wealth count for the poor in many ways. Yet, I see to-day that spiritually, I should have been better off without it, if the labor which helped earn it, could have had a more equal share. Co-operation would have made hundreds of homes happy. The gain of one man through the labor of others, establishes a thought-power, incompatible with the true idea of national equality."

Spiritual Congress and Parliament.

"May I ask you if this Congress over here, has come to any definite conclusion as a body.?"

"No, if it had, its power would have been felt more on the earthly side. Sometimes it seems almost wasted time—all their resolves and all their determination to act upon the statesmen of the world. The English Parliament also, on this side, is trying to influence its own country, as are the political devotees of all countries and nations; but what we really accomplish is so small compared with our hopes, that in seems hardly worth the trial. We see some one there who is bright with original thought, and think he may be a power for good. We give him the best help we can. He is inspired to make a speech which echoes through the nation : he receives a nomination, gets in with platforms which demand such extreme measures, that our power is lost. The forces are divided, and we fall back to devise other means for financial adjustment in the nation we have loved and love still."

"Will you keep on working?"

"O, yes. I think we will. Don't you think it best?"

"Yes," I answered. "I keep working, but it is in a direction far different from yours. I shall not give up. You do the work and I will report what you do. That is my work."

"Now, husband," said my wife, "you wrong yourself. You are doing something all the time. I would not say that if I were in your place."

"I was only a mill to grind out the news."

"Such a mill is very necessary," said Mr. Stanford, "and your husband, through his power of description, has done more to mould public opinion than resolutions or sermons."

I thanked him for his kind compliment and wondered if I was worthy of it.

"I'm a little disappointed in heaven," said my wife, after we had returned home. "It seems full of planning and striving, and reaching out—full of talking to people who wont hear you—full of different opinions—full of trying to get some one out of difficulties whom you wouldn't help when we were in earth life. When I think it over, I wonder what it means?"

"It means," I replied, "that you are in a spiritual world which is a neighbor not far removed from the earth world, and therefore, the duties neglected in that life, press upon us here, and we shall have to work our way up."

A little later, she came to me and said, "Its a great improvement on the old life. I just for a moment became burdened with the thought of the struggle of the old life and felt the shadow over here."

"I was afraid it would not be best for you to go with me."

"O, well, I'm glad I went, but Mr. Stanford is so intense, I quite felt that I must do something and didn't know what."

"You are doing all the time. Work for a while at the simpler problems, until you can understand great issues and their needs, and not be dragged down into the mists."

S. BOWLES.

PAPER XVI.

Dedication of Gen. Grant's Monument as seen from the Spirit Side of Life.

It is not often that any one event in the earth-world will serve to attract such multitudes from the heavenly world as did the Grant celebration in New York.

No king of any realm, no emperor of any country, would have touched the hearts of the multitude as this unpretending warrior of those days of long remembered strife. Washington, La Fayette, Lincoln and Garfield paid their tributes to the living Grant, while the hundreds of thousands of soldiers and people paid tributes to the dead warrior.

In the earth world when any great event is to transpire, months are consumed in the arrangements. Money is spent like water spilled, and invitations are debated over as though they were to give a place in Congress, instead of a seat of honor and a chance to say a few words on such an occasion. Then the heart burnings and bitterness of those who have no place in parade or on the platform, is something to be remembered for the years to come.

Over here it is different. Those most likely to be interested in such things here, know by a kind of heavenly instruction, their place and what it is best to do. The common soldier, if he felt the emotions which are almost divine, and wished to give utterance to noble thoughts, would be listened to as courteously as the most renowned general.

When I say that millions of spirits gathered there that day to witness that act of respect to the noble brother, I am not saying anything amiss, and there were veteran soldiers who had just come to the "land of the soul," who were given just as great respect as the noble men who directed their footsteps.

Words of General Grant.

"I hope the boys will get as near me as they can," said Grant, as he looked lovingly at the vast numbers of people gathered together, and then in most simple but pathetic words he said, "Boys, this is your day. That vast assemblage is here to do honor to those who helped to make my life what it was. It was your inspiration, your courage, your willingness to die, rather than give up, your unerring aim and valiant deeds that helped to lay my old worn out body in this grand receptacle.

Even now, boys, if the money used, could go to your children or your children's children, and help to make them happy and their lives beautiful, I would be content with no other honors paid me save those that come to the boys' thoughts as they read the history of the past.

I am chided a little by my noble companions for my want of appreciation of this great token of respect; but I repeat, that I can only take comfort in the fact, when I realize that this tribute includes every footsore and weary soldier, who gave his strength and life for the preservation of the Union."

Grant withdrew himself from the company that he was in, and swiftly and silently went with his family to the tomb. He came back rather saddened, than made happy, and said her thought was, "Oh, my husband, would that you could know the honor paid you this day;" and said he, "I could not break down the barriers sufficiently to let her know that I did know, that I was not dead, that all was plain to me. Will my own still have to wait until they reach this side to learn this truth, that 'Love cannot lose its own?' I wonder much about it."

He was told that persistent effort on his part might break down the barriers and make his family able to know the truth.

WORDS OF PRESIDENT LINCOLN.

Lincoln with the same kindly, loving smile that characterized him in that life, in a conversational

way, remarked, "My friend and brother, the means
which you feel had better have been appropriated
for the families or descendants of the soldiers, would
not have found its way to their homes. Indeed had
it been divided, it would have been but little per
capita. But I glory in this expression of the love of
a nation to its heroes. Had not your wisdom directed, your boys could never have fought the battles.
There was a power within yourself that was the
prime mover in the glory of a nation. This expression is not for the children of to-day, but when hundreds of years have passed, still will the steps of the
children of earth be turned toward this indestructi-
ble monument, and the children of that time will
learn lessons of valor, lessons of courage from the
inspiration, gained by those who tread on what
seems hallowed ground. And after not one rem-
nant of the old form is left, this tomb will be the
Mecca of the hero worshiper and the discouraged
children of future generations. Its lessons shall be
so broad that they will breathe forth of arts of peace
instead of arts of war.

But that which helps to build any foundation
of permanancy, must be recognized as the strong
hold of a prosperous people."

WORDS OF GENERAL WASHINGTON.

Then Washington spoke briefly. "The bells
still toll on every boat as it passes the resting place
of my body on the old Potomac; and little children
in cabin or on deck, ask the reason why. They
get then and there, their first lessons of the birth of
a great nation through great losses and much blood-

shed. Men raise their hats and think good thoughts for a little time, while tender woman, mayhap, pays her tribute in a tear. It is honest recognition, not hero worship, which will always be helpful to the American Republic."

Many others made short speeches, and the informal gathering broke up. Each went to his home; not with the tramp of feet which keep time to martial music, but silently, as spirits go, without fear of the crowd, or wondering about their welcome home, glad of the rest which home will bring us.

I hear some questioner ask, "Do you get tired there." I reply, "Yes, at times, the same as you do, when you say, 'I'm tired of thinking.' But rest comes surely, and you do not have to linger over the thoughts which come from fear of death or loss of home, as in earth life."

S. BOWLES.

PAPER XVII.
MY WIFE'S TRANSITION.

Years ago, when this life was new to me, when its beauties and possibilities made me feel that I had only just begun to live—when my freedom from physical pain seemed like a wondrous reprieve—when I at first, in fact, for some time, handled my new body with great care, fearing a return of the pain which cramped me, and of the weakness which crippled me, I wrote to you of earth, of my passing out and of my home over here.

If dying gave us all the wisdom which ignorant Spiritualists think it does, I could have seen at the beginning, how that message would have been received, but I did not. It was a history of my experiences, from me—Samuel Bowles—as much from myself as was every editorial I had ever written for the paper I had grown to love. *

But, you know how it was received. The great world, or those who paid any attention to it, said, "Well, if such a thing is possible, if one can send a message from the other world, may be he wrote it:" while others antagonized the idea, calling the thought expressed, the style utterly unlike me.

I persevered, however, for I saw seed taking root and growing, which was very encouraging. This moved me to keep on writing. The reason why I have not written more, is because I could not get access to this Instrument, as I desired to, and could find no other so well suited for my work.

With us over here, days do not drag. There is work and pleasure, and in fact, work is pleasure. Yet all my work and all the new scenes shown me, did not in the least wean me from my tender watchfulness over my dear wife.

We are not limited here as there. We keep the windows of the soul open, and therefore, her needs were readily recognized by me; and all I could do to aid her, was done. Yet we of this realm of light, are not unmixed with a little of selfishness.

Our love was more spiritual than human, therefore it lived. I wanted all her doubt removed that she should be in this higher life, beyond the possibility of physical pain. I wanted my Mary to come to me, yet I did not want to rob my son until he had learned there was no such thing as death.

---

* The Springfield (Mass.) Republican.

There have come to him some such glimpses, for the pulpit and the press have conceded many points which before were called impossible. Still his mind has not been as thoroughly imbued with the idea as it will be when he enters into the spiritual realm of thought as broadly as are his present ideas of the mortal world.

Mary could not understand, when the premonitions came of her final release, how she could feel so at rest in her mind. The dawn was nearer her eyes than she knew. Gradually, day by day she felt like giving up the battle of life and joining the hosts of the immortals. Her dreams became pictures of the old life, with father and mother, young again. Scenes of the old home were revived in memory. There were those to whom she talked of me, and of the possibility that after all I might have written that which was claimed for me.* "Its beautiful, any way," she said. How she cherished every sentiment she read anywhere of this life, its reunions, its embowered homes.

Transition of Mary Schermerhorn Bowles.

She could not feel serious dread of the change. I do not wish to recall too forcibly the scenes of the earth side, either before or after dissolution, but to describe as nearly as I can, the scene with us, when we, a loving band were waiting for her to bid good by to her body. She heard our singing; her mortal lips could not join in the song nor give a sign. Her spiritual vision was opened so she no longer felt doubt about the journey. The inner consciousness recognized the revelations spread out before her

---

* The Bowles Pamphlets. See cover.

view; and when the thread of life was snapped and she found herself in my arms, she said, "*Oh; hold me closely, Samuel, it must be a beautiful dream, and I shall have to go back!*"

Her mother, young and beautiful, tried to assure her, but she still had doubts of its being "real heaven." "There are so many young folks here it must be a dream," said she.

"You're young yourself, Mary," I said, as I led her where she could view her spiritual body. "Do you see any marks of age or pain?" "No, not one!"

A great wonder was revealed in her inquiring eyes, and admiration for the clothing which fell in soft folds about her.

"How did I get this new life in so short a time? Where was the dark river? Where was the boatman? Where was the 'valley of shadows?'"

"All hidden, Mary," I said, as I gazed upon her. More than her old self was she to me in her spiritual loveliness. "That change which comes in the 'twinkling of an eye,' has come to you, my wife. You have dropped the outer and are revelling in the inner life."

As she recognized one of the friends she used to meet in the long ago, who had been severely afflicted she exclaimed, "Why! where are your crutches? I hardly knew you. How well you look!"

To another, who had passed away from conditions which had made her a great sufferer from the accumulation of adipose tissue, she said, "Its strange how I knew you, when you are so slight."

"You knew me because you knew my soul better than you did my body," responded her friend.

"When persuaded to rest, she was delighted with her surroundings. "Now I touch a couch don't I, Samuel, and these are real chairs? Move one up to me: I don't want to feel there is anything the matter with my brain." Looking at her hands, so smooth and white, she said, "Come here, dear; I want to see if I can pinch with them."

"Yes, you have me to pinch and your hands to pinch with," I said, laughing at her doubts. This is a real world, Mary—a tangible one, and your home is a real one; All and more than I ever described to the earth-world, is real and true : but rest, dear, you need it."

After a little while, she rejoined me and began to examine the fairy-like cottage I had chosen for our new life.

"Hush!" said she, "I saw down home then, can't we go there?"

"We can, dear, if you desire, but you would feel more keenly the grief—know more of the preparations for burial, and witness much which you do not need to see or to know unless you desire to."

MRS. BOWLES ATTENDS HER OWN FUNERAL.

She concluded to wait. At the funeral she said, "Oh! Samuel, see how pale and dead she looks, referring to the old body as though it was another person. "How kind of them to say all those beautiful things about that dead woman, is it not?" said she with tears in her eyes. "They don't know that I am listening."

J. G. Holland whispered to her, and said, "If only there was present, what you called a medium before you came over here, and that medium was in good condition, we could all be seen—the glory of our white-robed party in contrast to their sorrowful mourning party—if that medium's ears could hear, they would hear our song of triumph and their 'Some sweet day' would be drowned out in our hosannas, for we have reached the 'sweet day' when life's dream is not over, but just begun."

"Oh, we shall disturb them," said she; then sorfully, "I wish our boy wouldn't shed tears, nor any one else for that 'dead woman.'"

"Try to place yourself as that dead woman, knowing it is the old body you used. Can't you realize it yet?" I asked.

She shook her head sadly, for the meaning in all its fulness, of the laying aside the old, had not yet been fully realized by her. "I shall learn by and by what it is to be 'all new'" she said, and again looked at her hands, her feet, and then at the dear old friends.

As time passed she began to realize the fulness of the new birth, and she joined me in the active pursuits of my life. Still some of my work was not interesting to her, perhaps because in my earth life, I did not carry my burdens home, or desire to discuss very much with her, the issues of the day. I wanted rest, when I went home—rest from the old treadmill; and sometimes, with the terrible nervous strain upon me, I fear I did not give her much of an idea of rest, with me there.

"Never mind," said she, as I referred to the past. "I will soon climb up to your level of thought. If I am willing to reach up, you will be willing to reach down to me."

The freedom from care of the home, the way all heaven has of adjusting itself and fulfilling the requirements of the spiritual body, and yet to her as it was to me, this life is a source of astonishment.

"Everything real, with hard housework or unruly servants to oversee, left out, it is a great novelty," she said to me only a few hours ago when we were talking of a recent visit to our friends of your beautiful city. "Why couldn't God have made the earth the same way?"

"Why isn't a tree large to start with?" I asked her in return. "Why isn't an egg a chicken? Why isn't a baby-girl a woman? It is all growth, Mary. Growth is God: you have only had but few revelations yet."

Step by step, I tried to show her the different phases of life, both high and low. As we were passing along through a place where the sorrowful congregate and those who had such life experiences as made it impossible as yet to overcome them, she said, "Oh! Samuel, see these distressed people; and I have not a cent in my pocket to give them."

"Have you a pocket, Mary?" I asked.

"No, not even a pocket;"

"Well, you know the old saying, 'The shroud has no pocket," is fully realized here. These people have brought the memory of unhappy and sinful living with them. All the money of Christendom would not relieve them. They are hungry, ah, so hungry but it is the hunger of the soul.

"Can't I do them some good, can't I talk with them?"

"Yes, by and by, when you have learned more of our ways of doing effective work, but come, we will go to a more cheerful place," and quickly as we willed it, we were there. She, my beloved of my old life, is now more truly mine than ever, and our relations are those which keep alive the best aspirations of the past, and unite with present desires for an endless work of love.

The Revelator, thousands of years ago, tried to describe Heaven, and because of his dearth of language, and his appealing to the greed of men whose desires were all for gold and gems, described it as abounding in them—while if I try to describe it, my words like his, are only as withered leaves to the pure bud and blossom. My best spiritual thought takes on such earthly form, that the people there cannot discern as I pray they may, the difference between the earthly and the spiritual.

SAMUEL BOWLES.

www.ingramcontent.com/pod-product-compliance
Lightning Source LLC
Chambersburg PA
CBHW030403170426
43202CB00010B/1471